GOOD · OLD · DAYS ®

We Survived— And Thrived ™

Edited by Ken and Janice Tate

HOUSE of
WHITE
BIRCHES
PUBLISHERS
SINCE 1947

We Survived–And Thrived™

Editors: Ken and Janice Tate
Managing Editor: Barb Sprunger
Associate Editor: Kelly Keim
Editorial Assistant: Joanne Neuenschwander
Copy Editors: Michelle Beck, Nicki Lehman, Mary Martin, Läna Schurb
Assistant Editors: Marla Freeman, Marj Morgan, June Sprunger

Publishing Services Manager: Brenda Gallmeyer
Graphic Arts Supervisor: Ronda Bechinski
Cover Design/Production Artist: Erin Augsburger
Traffic Coordinator: Sandra Beres
Production Assistants: Janet Bowers, Chad Tate
Photography: Tammy Christian, Christena Green, Kelly Heydinger
Photography Assistant: Linda Quinlan
Photography Stylist: Tammy Nussbaum

Chief Executive Officer: John Robinson
Publishing Director: David McKee
Marketing Director: Shirrel Rhoades
Book Marketing Director: Craig Scott
Editorial Director: Vivian Rothe
Publishing Services Director: Brenda Wendling

Printed in the United States of America
First Printing: 2003
Library of Congress Number: 2002107205
ISBN: 1-59217-002-1

Good Old Days Customer Service: (800) 829-5865

Every effort has been made to ensure the accuracy of the material in this book.
However, the publisher is not responsible for research errors or typographical mistakes in this publication.

We would like to thank the following for the art prints used in this book.

For fine-art prints and more information on the artists featured in *We Survived—And Thrived*, contact:

Apple Creek Publishing, Hiawatha, IA 52233, (800) 662-1707

Curtis Publishing, Indianapolis, IN 46202, (317) 633-2070, www.curtispublishing.com

Jim Daly, P.O. Box 25146, Eugene, OR 97402, caroledaly@earthlink.net

Mill Pond Press Inc., Venice, FL 34292, (800) 535-0331

John Sloane, Kirkland, IL 60146, (815) 522-6162

Wild Wings Inc., Lake City, MN 55041, (800) 445-4833

Dear Friends of the Good Old Days,

A few months after the death of my father, Janice and I were helping my mother with the painful task of going through "old things." Mama asked that I come to help her with the lifting and Janice to help her with the crying.

As we went through the accumulation of their life together, I found an old ledger in a dust-coated box in the top of one of the closets. Opening it, I found a mute witness of the tough times they faced when I was a child.

The oddest thing about looking through that old ledger, however, was the fact I don't remember those days as tough or grim, despite the hard, cold facts in front of me. There is an old proverb from those days that "at the end of the money there was a lot of month left." I saw that cycle repeated again and again. Daddy would be paid, but our little family was already in arrears at the general store. So part of Daddy's pay went to catch us up there, then to buy other provisions. We would have a surplus for a little while, but then the cycle would repeat itself.

But those weren't bad times! They were good times, punctuated with a lot more laughter than tears. In the midst of today's affluence, I find myself longing for the days when Mama's make-do meal of chicken and dumplings or cornbread and beans was the height of fine cuisine, and when a slab of her apple pie or peach cobbler was the *piece de resistance*.

With Mama's permission, I kept that old ledger as a reminder of my own roots— the deep, hard-working roots of my father and the tough yet tender roots of my mother.

When Janice and I first talked about putting together this special book for you, I realized that I had, at arm's length, the structure of *We Survived—And Thrived*. I reached up on my bookshelf and pulled down the old ledger and thumbed through its yellowed pages again.

In it I rediscovered that we had everything but money. We didn't know we were poor because the good Lord had given us strong backs and good imaginations. We learned the art of making ends meet through the old Depression-era proverb: "Use it up, wear it out, make it do, or do without." When times really got bad, we had loving neighbors to give a helping hand. And we had each other; it was that deep-rooted love that always held us together.

Those Good Old Days of old taught us that life is more than hard biscuits and water gravy. They taught us that, with tenacity and ingenuity and hard work and love, we could overcome every adversity. We could win every battle. We could take every punch thrown at us by life. And through it all we could survive—and thrive.

Ken Tate

❧ Contents ❧

We Didn't Know We Were Poor • 84

Making Ends Meet • 110

Love Held Us Together • 136

The Neighbors by Robert K. Abbett, courtesy of Wild Wings Inc.

We Had Everything But Money

Chapter 1

When I think back to the tough days of my childhood, I don't think of the things we didn't have. Oh, it would be easy in today's world to talk of privation, but the fact is, we had everything but money. Looking around the little cabin we called home, you might be surprised to hear that. But when I think of all we did have, I realize how blessed we really were.

We didn't have money to get our meat from a butcher; in fact, living out on the farm, we were about 10 miles from the nearest one. But we had plenty of room for a couple of cows and a few pigs. That supplied us with most of the protein we youngsters consumed until we were grown.

Mama and her widowed mother kept laying hens, and that kept us in eggs for cooking and pullets for the frying pan. The hens were productive enough for Grandma to sell for a few cents a dozen, or to barter for goods we couldn't produce for ourselves.

My morning wake-up call back then was the old rooster cockadoodling at the first hint of dawn. If the crowing didn't get you stirring, the threat of a splash of cold water did. We didn't have money for an alarm clock, but who needed one? Today I still don't need one to get out of bed in the morning.

Speaking of alarms, we sure didn't have money for a security system for the house, even if such a contraption had existed back then. We had no more than old hook-and-eyes for the screen doors. I'm not sure why anyone would have thought to break into our humble home, but if they had, the bellowing of our trusty hound Babe would have given us ample warning.

Babe was also worth his weight in gold out in the field, sniffing out rabbits and squirrels to put in the pot and add to the table. And to a country boy several miles removed from playmates, that hound was fellow adventurer, ally and confidante all rolled up in one.

I could go on and on about all we had. The nearby forest that provided wood-fire warmth when money couldn't buy coal or gas. The blackberry, strawberry and huckleberry vines that gave us assorted flavors of pies when we couldn't buy assorted flavors of ice cream. The rich, black earth for growing in our garden almost everything we needed to cook for today and can for tomorrow.

We had imagination when faced with "nothing to do." We had ingenuity when faced with hardship. And—in those rare instances when hard work and good fortune failed us—we had love and faith to sustain us through the toughest of times. Yes, we had everything but money.

—Ken Tate

Sewing Room by Doug Knutson, courtesy of Apple Creek Publishing

Feed Sacks & Love

*How she wanted a dress
no one else had ever worn!*

By Ellen M. Dearman

esides the heat, the dust and the interminable flies, August meant school was just around the corner. Oh, how we looked forward to school! Even though it was just a little country school and we went nowhere near a town, it was a big deal just to get away from the house for a few hours a day. Besides the opportunity to learn, there would be other children to visit with at recess. We even welcomed a chance to see the school bully and the little rich girl who was so stuck-up.

Yes, we looked forward to school, but we also dreaded it, for we were so very poor. There was never enough money to buy new clothes to start school. We had only castoffs and hand-me-downs, passed on to us by our cousins in town who were just a little bit better off than we were. How often I begged Mama for just one dress that nobody else had ever worn! And how often she told me I should be grateful for what I had and not beg for more! Being a mother now myself, I can appreciate the marvelous patience Mama showed when I pestered her for new clothes. I know she wanted me to have them, but eating was important, too, and there just wasn't anything leftover for new clothes.

One August, Mama sent all of us to my grandmother's house in town for a weekend. What a thrill! At Grandma's we could actually go to the toilet indoors, and water came right out a pipe in the bathroom!

That Saturday we headed for the last building on Main Street, the social center of the small town, a building that was more important than even the bank or post office—the feed store.

One learned things at the feed store. Gathered around the old rusty pop box, tilted back in the sagging cane-bottomed chairs, we learned who was getting married, who was having a baby, who had been sent to the hospital with chest pains or gallbladder trouble.

At last the man who owned the feed store and his hefty, jolly wife noticed us kids, and my grandmother introduced us. They were happy to meet "Peggie's young-uns" and ceremoniously threw back the lid of the pop box, inviting us to have a "sody water." Excited, we crowded around, gazing with wonder at the array of drinks nestled in the chipped ice, sparkling and twinkling in jewel-bright colors—amethyst and emerald and ruby and onyx. After finally making our decisions, we heard the tantalizing "Pop! Fizzzzz!" as the caps were pried off the thick bottles. Then, sipping the nectar slowly, we savored the rare treat. We thought we were in heaven.

Seeing that the younger kids were being good and quiet, at least for the time it took to drink their sody water, I wandered down the long aisles of the feed store, exploring.

Feed stores have such a special place in my memory. The odor especially remains with me even now. All the different types of grain—corn, oats and wheat; the molasses, dark and rich, that was used to make sweet feed for horses and calves; and the salt and mineral blocks all combined to create an aroma that is like nothing else in this world.

It was dim and cool back in the store. Way in the back, among the stacks and stacks of 50-pound feed sacks, I spied a mama cat with a litter of kittens. (Feed stores always kept a cat, for all the grains and seeds around made a haven for rats and mice.) I discovered all sorts of other things as I wandered, such as tack for horses, cattle prods, medications of all sorts, poisons and fertilizers. Big burlap bags—"tow sacks"—of grains and seeds were stacked on wooden pallets along the walls. In one corner were stacked 25-pound sacks of garden seeds that were sold in bulk or by the pound. These sacks were not just plain burlap, but printed cotton, in a variety of florals and prints and checks of all colors. I thought those feed sacks were lovely. How I wished I could have a dress made from one of those!

I was finished with my drink but reluctant to return the bottle to the wooden crate of empties. Then I heard my grandmother calling. It was time to go.

Late Sunday evening, Daddy arrived to take us home. We were eager to get back for we had missed Mama something fierce. Mama was our mainstay, and two nights without her tucking us in and singing us lullabies in her rich, sweet tenor seemed like an eternity.

When we got home we burst into the house, anxious to tell Mama all about our weekend in town. All of us tried to talk at once and tripped over each other in our clumsy attempts to give her a hug. I looked and looked at her until I was satisfied that she was still the same Mama we had left on Friday evening.

Then I turned my attention to our home, to make sure nothing about it had changed either. But something had changed, for I immediately noticed a difference. I saw something that told me Mama had had a very good reason for sending us away for the weekend. I saw Mama's Singer in the living room.

Mama usually kept her Singer in her bedroom, with a lace doily and pictures of us kids and Daddy on top of it. Mama had got the Singer from her mother, and it was a beauty. The black wrought-iron treadle gleamed and the rich wood of the cabinet glistened.

On this hot August Sunday evening, as I stood there looking at the Singer, all folded up and ready to be rolled back into Mama's room,

Mama usually kept her Singer in her bedroom, with a lace doily and pictures of us kids and Daddy on top of it. Mama had got the Singer from her mother, and it was a beauty. The black wrought-iron treadle gleamed and the rich wood of the cabinet glistened.

I knew she had been up to something good. I could hardly wait to see the results of her labors.

I didn't have to wait long, for as soon as everyone had settled down a little, Mama told us to sit down, for she had a surprise for us. I sat, fidgety, impatiently, as she presented to my littlest sister a brand-new dress. We "oohed" and "ahhed" over it, and of course she had to model it right then and there, proud as a peacock.

Next were shirts for the two youngest boys, one apiece, but made of the same material so as not to have any arguments. Then there was a dress for the middle sister. That took care of the kids who weren't going to school yet. Next Mama brought out two shirts for the two oldest boys, again made of the same fabric, and my, how they strutted as they modeled those shirts!

By this time, my palms were sweaty and I could hardly sit still, so eager was I to see what Mama had made for me. At last! At last! I held my breath as Mama disappeared into her bedroom. It seemed she was gone forever, but at last she reappeared, bearing not one, not two, but *three* brand-new dresses that nobody had ever worn before! I was in heaven.

There couldn't have been a prouder little girl in the whole world than I was on the first day of school that year. I felt like a princess! Not even the stuck-up little rich girl could steal my thunder *that* day, for I had brand-new clothes. And they hadn't been bought in any old store where thousands of other people had seen and handled them first. Mine had been handmade with lots of love and care and, the most important ingredient, feed sacks.

The feed-store man had saved the sacks and sold them to Mama for a quarter apiece. She had carefully taken out the seams, washed the yard of material and put it away, saving it until she had enough of the same pattern to make a dress. Then, without even a printed paper pattern to go by, she had lovingly created the dresses that I was so proud to wear. I learned these details years later when I was grown and reminiscing about those special dresses.

It brings me special joy to remember that first day of school, when I was clad in the richest of garments, created by Mama on her old Singer, out of feed sacks. ❖

Depression Flour-Sack Underwear

When I was just a maiden fair,
Mama made our underwear;
With many kids and Dad's poor pay,
We had no fancy lingerie.
Monograms and fancy stitches
Did not adorn our Sunday britches;
Pantywaists that stood the test
Had "Gold Medal" on my breast.
No lace or ruffles to enhance;
Just "Pride of Bloomington" on my pants.
One pair of panties beat them all,
For it had a scene I still recall—
Harvesters were gleaning wheat
Right across my little seat.
Rougher than a grizzly bear
Was my flour-sack underwear,
Plain, not fancy, and two feet wide,
And tougher than a hippo's hide.
All through Depression each Jill and Jack
Wore the sturdy garb of sack.
"Waste not, want not"; we soon learned
That a penny saved is a penny earned.
There were curtains and tea towels, too,
And that is just to name a few.
But the best beyond compare
Was my flour-sack underwear.

By Morris W. Jones

The 99-Cent Model A

He desperately needed a car, but he had no money. Then fate intervened.

By Charles Davis

During the depths of the Great Depression, I attended a junior college in the Midwest. I had no wheels and the daily round-trip hike was more than five miles. Six months before, I had sold a 1929 Pontiac roadster for $15 to help pay for my tuition. Now I was desperate for any kind of transportation. There was no bus line along my route; I was so impoverished that I would have had to pass anyway. I had long ago given up asking my parents for money.

My father was a piano teacher and half of his students paid for their lessons in kind. There were sacks of vegetables, meat from the local butcher and haircuts. I spent a pleasant hour or two every week having a trim and shampoo. But this indulgence came to an abrupt end when it was discovered that my father owed the barber.

Once in awhile my mother would slip me a dime so I could join the gang at a Saturday-night movie, but that was it. When I approached my father for a little cash, he stared at me in disbelief and then averted his eyes. So how was I ever going to get money for another car?

Being afoot was bad for several reasons. Most of the heavy industry and shops were located down in the river bottoms; a slim chance of employment might exist there, but that was miles from where I lived. A steady girlfriend was out of the question, too; any kind of recreation depended on a few buddies who were fortunate enough to own or have access to an automobile.

About halfway between home and school was a new-car agency. Adjacent to the showroom was the company used-car lot overflowing with unsold vehicles. It was a few blocks out of my way to walk by, but the urge to eye their selection and imagine myself tooling along behind the wheel was strong enough to justify the detour.

My favorite was a 1930 Ford Model A sport business coupe with a soft top and a rumble seat. Nearly every day I would stroll around it for a long time and dream. I was always at the wheel, usually with a cute girl at my side, a couple in the rumble seat and perhaps another twosome cuddling up front. Once when I was standing there right in the middle of a pleasant vision, a thoughtless buddy who was familiar with my financial situation drove by and destroyed my fantasy by yelling, "Eat your heart out!"

In a shrill, tremulous voice, I made my request. "A dollar! All I need is one dollar!" Blurting out all of the pertinent details (the extra penny was for sales tax), I waited breathlessly for a response.

The Love of My Life by John Slobodnik, House of White Birches nostalgia archives

The asking price for "my car" was $80. It might as well have been $8,000.

Occasionally I would check everything on the lot. Nothing was moving. Many of the cars had been there for more than a year.

I finally made up my mind to omit the side trips and spare myself the pain of having to turn away after my delusions of grandeur. But one day, as I made my way home and passed a beam of the agency, my feet began to drag. *One more last look.* I changed my course.

From a block away I could see a large sign-board that had been erected in front of the lot. I quickened my pace. As the word "SALE" came into view, I began to run. A sizeable crowd had gathered and was intent on the dramatic proc-lamation displayed below.

"This is a 99-cent sale. All of the cars on this lot will be sold starting at 8 o'clock in the morning. First come, first served. The sale price of each car is on the windshield."

About halfway between home and school was a new-car agency. It was a few blocks out of my way to walk by, but the urge to eye their selection and imagine myself tool-ing along behind the wheel was strong enough to justify the detour.

The cars had been moved about and I did not see the Model A. My throat started to con-tract as I climbed onto the running board of the nearest car and frantically began to search. The most expensive ones were in front; some of them were less than a year old, and they were priced at $99.99. As the rows of cars moved back, the prices decreased according to vintage.

Feeling faint, I grabbed a radiator ornament for support. I had spotted mine! It was in the last row and the sale price stood out clearly on the windshield—99 cents! I lit out for home.

When I rushed into the house, everyone was in the living room. My father was flipping the pages of his newspaper and my mother, as usual, was mending something. Grandma had arrived the day before from out of town and was still sorting out personal belongings. I stood in the center of the room, trying to speak, but gasping and wheezing from my run. No one looked up.

In a shrill, tremulous voice, I made my request. "A dollar! All I need is *one dollar*!" Blurting out all of the pertinent details (the extra penny was for sales tax), I waited breathlessly for a response. My mother looked up, eyed me for a few seconds (I believe with pity), glanced quickly at my father and returned to her stitching. My father rattled the paper, squinted and appeared to concentrate harder on something he was reading. Grandma continued to sort.

I was desperate. But any arguments that I thought were reasonable were soon reduced to caterwauling.

Then, for the first time in many years, I began to cry. A child can cry and get away with it. Even an adult, under the assault of some painful emotion, can shed tears and it seems natural. But there is something awful and even disgusting when a 19-year-old fellow does it. A young buck with a wretched, tear-streaked face, blubbering and gag-ging? Revolting! But I was seeking compassion.

It worked. Grandma got up and walked over to me. She didn't take me in her arms, wipe my tears or utter one word of solace. In her hands she had an old leather snap pocketbook. She opened it (I can still hear the *snap),* drew out a crumpled dollar bill and hand-ed it to me. "Go git yourself that car, Babe." Then she went back to her business.

Still sniffing, I was out of the house in a jiffy, but I flung the door back open and yelled, "Thanks, Grandma!" I gave my parents a quick glance. There was no change in their activities except that my father's mouth was slightly puck-ered and my mother seemed to be applying her needle with more energy.

In minutes I was in front of the car lot and pushing my way through a growing crowd to where my car was parked. I opened the door and slid into the seat, settled back, breathed a sigh of relief and closed my red eyes.

After awhile, a salesman came over and asked me why I was spending the afternoon in one of the company automobiles. I showed him the crumpled dollar bill I still clenched in my hand and told him that I fully understood the terms of the sale and it was my firm intention to be sitting in *this* car at 8 o'clock the following morning. And I wasn't going to move until the deal was signed, sealed and delivered.

He looked at his watch and shook his head. "That's 16 hours. I don't think the boss'll go for it."

I was allowed to sweat for an hour before the owner appeared, accompanied by the salesman. He looked me over for a minute, then asked what I did. I told him I was a student at the local junior college, but I didn't let it go at that. He patiently heard me out—the tedious and exhausting round-trip by foot (which wasn't helping my studies any), the difficulty of finding a job without a car, and Grandma. I showed him the dollar.

He drew the salesman aside and they talked. Every now and then the salesman would nod. It seemed an eternity before they sauntered back. The boss was wearing a smile.

"We think it might be a good promotional idea for the sale, if you really plan to stick it out." I swore to him that I was glued to the car seat until 8 o'clock the next morning.

That evening, a reporter and a photographer from the local newspaper showed up with a scantily clad carhop from a drive-in across the street. On her serving tray was an enormous hamburger. I was famished. The boss was summoned and he and the carhop arranged themselves on opposite sides of the car door so that my pale, drawn face would be framed in the window.

The flashbulb went off and I reached for the sandwich, but my extended fingers collided with the back of the owner's hand. He had been quicker on the draw. Happily munching away, he chatted for a few minutes, then wandered off, leaving me to starve.

Except for brief periods of dozing, I did not sleep that night. Not only was I happy over the expectation of having wheels, but I was also very hungry.

Then, just before sunup, figures began scurrying among the cars, nearly all of them making a beeline for my Model A.

"Shucks! There's already somebody in it!"

At 8 o'clock sharp, a clerk appeared with a bill of sale and the title. I handed him the dollar and he presented me with the precious documents.

Within a few days, I found an after-school job delivering for a prescription pharmacy and had a steady girlfriend. I drove the A until Pearl Harbor, then sold it and joined the Air Force. Eventually I wore out the bill of sale showing it to people.

Recently I went to an antique car show where there were several Model A Fords on display and for sale. In splendid condition and original down to the spidery wire wheels was a 1930 sport business coupe. I found the owner and asked him how much he wanted for it. Without hesitating he said, "$16,500. Firm." ❖

Model A Standard Sport Roadster   Ford Showroom, from the collections of Henry Ford Museum and Greenfield Village.

Something Out of Nothing

By Helen Colwell Oakley

Back in the late 1920s and early 1930s, when I was a youngster, being thrifty was very much a part of the times. Pennies were counted and nothing was discarded until it was beyond salvaging.

Besides me, my family consisted of Dad, Mom, five sisters and four brothers. Dad was a good provider, but it took a lot of providing to keep all of us properly fed, clothed and housed. Nevertheless, my parents both worked hard to make our life a pleasant one.

I remember delightful times when Mom made something out of nothing. Sometimes she used something from the closet in the downstairs bedroom that she used for a sewing room. The little room was a catchall, with baskets of clothes waiting to be ironed and piles of clothes to be mended. It also was a good place to hide goodies until the proper time.

The closet in the little room was "heaped brimful and running over," as the old-timers would say, with used clothes and finery that Mom and our relatives had passed on to be used again. An old trunk was filled with old clothes, and other old garments were piled on shelves and stored with the ribbons, laces and doodads in old pillowcases. What fun it was to watch Mom haul out the fancy dresses and plush velvets from the closet when my sisters or I teased for a "new" dress or skirt for a special occasion.

Mom really got carried away with a beautiful, long, black skirt with gold and green lines

Mom made patchwork quilts from the scraps leftover from her sewing. Sometimes they were from new fabric but often they were not. It didn't matter, as long as they were bright and colorful.

down its full length. It had been hers long ago and she was particularly fond of it. We had been asking for something new to wear to the Christmas program in our little country schoolhouse, so she searched the closet and came up with the skirt. It didn't look like anything that would look good on little girls, so we weren't too enthusiastic. But there was a gleam in Mom's eyes. Maybe she would work her magic with the sewing machine and come up with something that wouldn't be too bad.

After ripping out the seams, cleaning and pressing the material, she was all set to go on her new project. Draping fabric on the dining-room table, she got out her large shears and began snipping. Three adorable black skirts with rows of stripes came out of the material that had once been one. And each was different: on one, the rows of stripes were inside the pleats; on another, the stripes were on the outside, with the solid black inside the pleats. And my little sister's skirt had the stripes running horizontally.

When we wore our "new" skirts with fresh white blouses and tiny black bows to the school entertainment, we felt like fairy princesses and received many compliments. Mom's "something out of nothing" had made us very happy. It made Mom happy, too, for she took great pride in making do. If she wanted something, she got busy looking for a way to provide it without having to buy it brand new.

She could come up with almost anything we wanted, whether it was a petticoat or extra fruit jars or perhaps a hat to wear to a funeral. She would search the house, and if she didn't have what we wanted, she would suggest something else. There wasn't much money around in those times, and Mom said it was foolish to squander money on something new when you could make do with what you already had. She salvaged clothing by passing it down until it was really shot. If our boots were sometimes too large, she said that they were better that way. In fact, I still think everyone should buy boots several sizes too large, as I remember Mom saying, "The bigger the better."

Mom made patchwork quilts from the scraps leftover from her sewing. Sometimes they were from new fabric but often they were not. It didn't matter, as long as they were bright and colorful. Pajamas were sometimes made from the good parts of worn-out sheets, and tablecloths that were beginning to show wear could be used for dinner napkins. Large bath towels and hand towels made nice washcloths when the ends frayed. Worn parts were cut from large blankets and sheets and presto! There were the makings of a crib sheet or blanket. With the addition of a colorful binding, it looked like a brand-new blanket, for only a few pennies.

Mom made new coats out of old coats. Taking a coat that had been one of the aunts', she would begin cutting in the early morning and, by nightfall, come up with a child's beautiful coat with matching leggings and hat, ready except for the finishing touches—buttonholes, buttons and tacking on a little fur collar.

Feed bags made dish towels. The colorful printed ones were used for pretty aprons, luncheon sets, blouses, housedresses and children's pants and shirts. Sometimes there was a calamity when Mom started making a garment out of a feed bag and it looked like there wouldn't be enough fabric. She would get on the crank telephone and call around to see if anyone else had the same color and pattern. Feed bags were traded around the neighborhood quite frequently in those days.

At Christmastime, Mom would make baby bibs from discarded towels, adding colorful

I remember delightful times when Mom made something out of nothing. Sometimes she used something from the closet in the downstairs bedroom that she used for a sewing room.

bindings around the edges. She would turn out colorful pot holders from scraps. Pillow tops were made from circles of satin, taffeta and flowered crepe. They were beautiful, and almost every home had one on the parlor sofa.

Almost everything went into her rag rugs when it could no longer be used for anything else. We could pick out the fabric from a favorite dress, blouse or skirt as we looked at the finished product on the floors of our old farmhouse.

Mom salvaged our discarded dolls, too. She would patch them up and add a perky new outfit, and soon the doll would be back in some little girl's arms.

Mom was handy with a hammer and nails, as well as a saw. She often repaired forgotten sleds, wagons and other toys for our younger cousins or the neighborhood kids. They were as proud of the secondhand stuff as they would have been of new toys from the stores in town or the Sears, Roebuck and Co. or Montgomery catalogs.

If a kid didn't have a rope for his or her hand sled, Mom would cut off a chunk from one of her older clotheslines that had been stored in the back room in case of an emergency. Jump ropes for my sister, girlfriends and neighborhood pals came off Mom's old clotheslines, too.

One day a neighbor lady wheeled her baby over in a baby carriage. When Mom saw that she didn't have a warm baby blanket, Mom cut a chunk out of an old blanket from her rag bag and zipped it up on the sewing machine in nothing flat. It looked like new and did the trick. She even brought out an old net curtain to protect the baby from the flies and mosquitoes.

No matter who came to our house, if they had a hole in their shoe or boot, Mom would search the house until she came up with a pair that would fit. And if a sweater or stocking cap or mittens were called for, Mom would supply them!

Mom taught us how to make sewing baskets and tote bags out of empty oatmeal boxes by gluing pretty scraps of fabric to the outside of the boxes. Velvet scraps glued onto candy boxes made attractive holders for jewelry or keepsakes. Pincushions of all sizes and shapes were

Something New 'Most Every Day, 1927 Singer Sewing Machine Ad

easy projects for beginners. Mom would make a pattern and our small fingers would try to follow the outline, snipping until it looked just right, then basting and finally sewing. Last came the trimming, sometimes with bits of lace.

Rainy or frigid, snowy days brought out the best in Mom's creativity, perhaps to keep us busy while we were shut up indoors so that she could peacefully get some of her endless household chores out of the way. It always did her heart a world of good to see "something out of nothing"! ❖

Finding the Perfect Tree by Lee Stroncek, courtesy of Wild Wings Inc.

The Christmas Without Money

By Benita Davidson

I grew up during the Great Depression of the 1930s. Even in those difficult days, Christmas was a special time for our family. But one yuletide stands out above all the others in my memory.

We were living in the Upper Piedmont near Spartanburg, S.C., at Beaumont Mill Village where my daddy was a textile worker. But the mill was curtailing; he only worked two or three days every other week. It was hard to feed and clothe a family of seven on that, so Mama made most of our clothing and household linens. She sewed for the public, too, to supplement our income. Fortunately, we never went cold or hungry or ragged, as many poor children did then.

Since we had no money for extras like presents, we made our own. But the holiday season was upon us before we knew it, and the prospect of celebrating Christmas looked slim.

Then Mama came up with a great idea. "We're going to have an old-fashioned Christmas this year," she announced, "just like we had when I was a child!" We were so excited! Our favorite pastime was listening to Mama's stories about growing up "back home" in the mountains of North Carolina.

The air was crisp, but we bundled up warmly. Loading the younger children onto my brother's red wagon, we headed for the nearby woods. There we found our Christmas tree, a shapely pine. We also gathered cedar and lots of holly with bright red berries.

Back home, Mama brought out a single string of lights (our first) and some shiny ornaments leftover from better times. We made more decorations. We thought ours was the most beautiful Christmas tree in the whole world!

Mama decorated the house with fragrant boughs of cedar and holly—over the mirrors and pictures, a spray on each mantelpiece, and a huge wreath for the front door, tied with a big red bow.

That afternoon, she baked a fresh coconut cake, a chocolate cake and some pumpkin pies. We cut out gingerbread boys and decorated them with raisins. The best part of it was eating the broken cookies afterward.

The next day, a U.S. Mail truck stopped in front of our house! It brought a box of red apples and a sack of black walnuts from Mama's uncle in North Carolina. Granny came early on Christmas Eve, bringing good things to eat from the farm. Mama roasted a big hen and fixed all the trimmings. She covered the table with a red checkered cloth and set out her best dishes and silverware.

When Daddy came home from work, the house smelled delicious. He carried a huge sack of oranges over his shoulder and held a big box of stick candy under his arm.

At 6 p.m., he brought in the Yule log and laid it on the fire with great ceremony. "Christmas will last until every bit of this log has burned to ashes," he told us. We hoped it would never go out.

I recall vividly the beauty of that night as we walked home from church with gifts under our arms. Then soft snow began to fall.

We gathered around the fireplace. Mama lit the old kerosene lamp that she and Daddy had started keeping house with, and set it on the mantelpiece. She read us the story of Christ's birth from the second chapter of the Gospel according to St. Luke. Then we sang Christmas carols for Daddy, hung our stockings by the fireplace and went to bed.

We were up before daybreak to see if Santa had visited us, and we found our stockings bulging with goodies. And beneath the tree we found beautifully dressed dolls in tiny beds, a handsome game table with a checkerboard painted right on it, a set of checkers and a tiny set of dishes. There was a new dress for each of us girls. Mine was red velvet!

The house was cold so Daddy got up and chased us back to bed until he could roust the fire. We took our stockings with us and feasted on the goodies. It's a wonder we weren't sick from eating fruit, candy and nuts on an empty stomach, but we were too happy to be sick.

Looking back now, I realize it took a lot of work for our parents to give us a big Christmas that year, but I'm sure it was a labor of love. Daddy had built the game table and doll beds long after we slept. Mama had sewed far into the night, fixing up our old dolls and making our new dresses from hand-me-downs.

Many a Christmas has come and gone since then; some of them were happy, some sad. We children grew up, married and scattered to the four winds: Louisiana, Georgia, Kentucky, Virginia, Washington, D.C., Michigan, Montana and even Japan.

We buried Granny in 1945 and Daddy and one grandchild in 1955.

During the intervening years, our greatest happiness was in receiving a card or letter or package from our loved ones so far away, or better yet, a phone call. How wonderful just to hear their voices!

In our own homes, we kept alive some of the traditions that our family started on that long-ago Christmas.

Now, the hand of fate has brought each of us back to South Carolina again. This year, we're planning an old-fashioned Christmas, just like the ones we had as children! We're making gifts for each other, and ornaments for the tree. We'll make gingerbread boys, too, and let the children help. We'll light that same old kerosene lamp and read the Christmas story from the family Bible. Then we'll sing carols and watch the Yule log glow.

But most of all, we'll remember that never-to-be-forgotten Christmas, when we were so poor money-wise, but wealthy beyond all comparison! ❖

Puzzling Payments

By Darryl E. Matter with Roxana Marie Matter

In 1933 the United States was in the midst of one of the worst depressions in history. Many people were unemployed. Foreclosures of homes, farms and businesses were commonplace. Banks were closing with increasing frequency. Although President Franklin Delano Roosevelt initiated many new programs designed to end the Depression, it would be several years before the economic situation improved.

Our family owned and operated a small department store during the 1920s and 1930s, and we all remember those Depression years well. In addition to the problems of unemployment and foreclosures, there were crop failures brought about by drought and dust storms. Then, too, there were the "bank holidays." An additional problem plagued many merchants: a serious shortage of coinage with which to make payments and make change.

Early in 1933 it seemed as though everyone suddenly became interested in jigsaw puzzles. (Assembling jigsaw puzzles had long been a popular form of recreation, but interest in them surged in 1933.) We always carried a few jigsaw puzzles in our store, but early in 1933 we found that we just couldn't keep up with the demand.

Jigsaw puzzles sold from about 10 cents up to several dollars each. There were countless subjects: landscapes, seascapes, portraits of famous people, reproductions of famous paintings, automobiles and airplanes. There was a subject to interest almost everyone. Some years later we read that more than 6 million jigsaw puzzles had been sold nationwide during the first few months of 1933, when interest was at its peak.

Because small change was in short supply and because jigsaw puzzles were so popular, we began to accept some jigsaw puzzles in exchange for merchandise. We knew that we would have no trouble selling them or exchanging them for other puzzles. Several other merchants in our town also accepted jigsaw puzzles, and we sometimes traded puzzles for their merchandise.

Several things demonstrated the popularity of jigsaw puzzles in our community at that time. One of our town's most prominent bachelors proposed to his girlfriend with a jigsaw puzzle. She had to assemble it to read his proposal. Not to be outdone, she had a jigsaw puzzle made that he had to assemble in order to read her acceptance!

A puzzle club was formed in our community; it sponsored contests for puzzle enthusiasts. And jigsaw puzzles were to be found in many restaurants and soda fountains, where they were provided for the entertainment of patrons. I remember well the puzzles we assembled over coffee in the drugstore next to our department store.

Before 1933 ended, many forms of "emergency money" were devised to take the place of the coins that were in such short supply. Several merchants in our town used paper scrip; others employed wooden nickels and tokens. In this way we managed to get along until coins became plentiful again. But none of that "substitute money" was as interesting to me as the jigsaw puzzles we used for barter and for change. ❖

The Chicken Salesman

By J.B. Cearley

I glanced at the angry sun that scorching day in late July 1933. I wiped the sweat from my forehead as I turned to face Mother. "It's too hot to clean out the chicken house," I tried to explain.

"It will only get hotter the longer you wait to start. We are going to clean it out now," she commanded.

"But why, with it so hot?" I continued to object, but I had already started for the horse lot to harness our mules, Joe and Red. I never could win an argument with Mother.

I harnessed the team, hitched them to the wagon and drove it to the chicken house. It was about 95 degrees in the shade as I got the big grain scoop and began cleaning the floor. I sweated profusely and swirling dust filled my nostrils as I labored in the broiling heat.

Mother came in and began to help me. When I saw how she was sweating, I suggested, "You go tend to your house chores and I'll take care of the chicken house."

Late that afternoon, I saw a country salesman driving along the road toward our house. I could spot one a mile away. They always drove old cars, invariably with a large chicken crate fastened onto the back.

"Then clean it real good, Son," she said kindly. "With things the way they are, we need to keep the chicken house clean and free of fleas and mites. Those eggs and our cream are all we have to sell to buy food."

Just then, Old Cackle, our sorry white rooster, came in, got scared and flew across the roost poles, stirring up a terrible-smelling dust storm. "Sorry old rooster," I complained. "We ought to eat that thing."

"Too old and tough," Mother said. "We have several hens that have quit laying. We'll catch the non-layers and sell them and Cackle next week."

I glanced outside where our flock of laying hens was trying to beat the heat under the windmill water tank and the three scraggly trees that stood near the chicken house. "Things are really bad. No one has a job or any money," I grumbled.

"When you get the floor cleaned, be sure to sprinkle plenty of lime everywhere," Mother instructed. "I want our hens to produce eggs, and they can't lay well if they are covered with fleas."

July and August on the high plains of Northwest Texas are sultry months, and they were especially hot during the Dust Bowl days in 1933. The new president had promised us a New Deal, but what we had was drought, poor crops and 5-cent cotton. I knew that my dad was a good farmer, but he could not make it rain enough to produce a crop. And even if he'd had a crop, he couldn't sell it for a decent price; no one could.

After sweating five or six gallons and bumping my head a dozen times on the roost poles, I had the chicken house clean. Then I got the sack of lime and sprinkled it generously over the roost and the floor. I was happy that the place looked so nice. I knew we needed every egg the hens could produce.

With the chicken house finished, I drove the team and wagon to the field and scattered the cleanings onto the land. It made excellent fertilizer.

Late that afternoon, I saw a country salesman driving along the road toward our house. I could spot one a mile away. They always drove old cars, invariably with a large chicken crate fastened onto the back.

I watched as the faded black 1938 Chevy rattled to a stop beside our house. I noted that the fellow was looking around, no doubt trying to figure out if he could gyp us out of something. Those fellows could skin a mule without disturbing the hair; they were even sharper with the average housewife.

The fellow got out of his car and lifted his arms to get a little air under his sticky shirt, then got his Watkins Products bag and a copy of a farm magazine he hoped to peddle to my folks.

Dad was sitting on the front porch, but the man turned to me as he said, "Your mother here, boy?"

At age 15, I hated it when someone called me "boy" in a derogatory manner. "I'm here, Dad's here, and my mother is here," I said a little sharply.

"Then tell your mother that I have a present for her," he instructed.

"Like what?" I asked sharply. I glanced at Dad; he was grinning. He didn't care too much for peddlers.

The man reached into his old sedan and picked up a large piece of paper. "This beautiful picture is free for your mother," he said.

The colorful autumn picture showed some Northeastern farm scene. All that beautiful color didn't resemble our Dust Bowl country. I didn't

say a word to the salesman, so he turned and walked toward the porch.

After bowing and speaking ever so politely to Dad, the man said, "I'm Henry Franklin, Sir. May I speak with your lovely wife? I have a present for her."

Mother came to the door and stared at the salesman.

"Good evening, Ma'am. Here," he said, handing her the picture, "is a gift just for you. Isn't that a pretty picture for your wall? Makes everything look so cheerful. Big 12- by 15-inch colored picture." The pictures were a come-on.

Mother took the picture, then stood sturdy and aloof as she faced Henry Franklin. This beanpole peddler wasn't related to Ben.

Henry displayed the magazine as he began his canned spiel. "I have this beautiful and most wonderful farm magazine that you folks need and want," he insisted.

"And why do we need that thing?" Mother quipped slyly.

Henry began to realize that he had met his match. "It has worlds of farm news, many fine poems about farm life, a fine business section for the farmer and lots of interesting stories and articles for you and your children. Every farmer in the country is subscribing to the magazine. It's the biggest and best bargain you can find anywhere," Henry insisted.

Mother eyed him boldly. "If every farmer in the country is buying one of those magazines from you, why are you driving around in that old wreck of a car with some sickly old chickens in a coop on back?" she asked. "You should be rich."

Henry gasped and turned to face his faded sedan. It seemed to be on its last leg. After a moment, he found his voice again. "Oh," he insisted, smiling like a new groom, "I love that old car." He changed his stance to show her his Watkins Products display case.

"I have many good bargains for you today."

"How much for a box of black pepper?"

I knew we were out of black pepper and would not drive our Model A the 16 miles to town until Saturday, our shopping day. We all liked the Watkins products, especially the black pepper. But when Franklin told her the price, Mother merely shrugged. "I can get it for half that price in town," she said. "Don't you know we're in a Depression?"

Henry seemed to wilt a little. "I'll trade you a subscription to the farm magazine and the black pepper for two chickens." He looked hopefully at her, then turned to smile at Dad, hoping for some support.

"I have high-quality laying hens," Mother told him. "I never consider parting with my hens. Best in the county."

I glanced toward our overheated laying hens, wondering if they were even average. What did Mother have in mind? And then, at that moment, Cackle walked into the yard, panting.

The exasperated Henry Franklin made a grand offer. "I'll trade you a magazine subscription for that rooster."

Mother seemed to grow a little as she eyed Henry and said, "I'll have you know that Cackle is a quality rooster. He's lost a few feathers in this heat, but he is a real fine rooster. And I don't want any dinky little box of pepper; I want that largest box. Understand?"

Henry stopped to swallow. He wasn't getting far with this poor farm wife. He glanced at Dad again for help and got none. Dad was merely grinning at the confrontation. Henry turned back to face Mom. "Could I interest you in some fine quality flavoring?" he asked. "You know that Watkins has only the finest extracts."

"Like what?" She stood firm, demanding.

"Well, now, I have strawberry, vanilla, cherry and lemon flavoring. They are all of the very best quality. And I have other things."

"For that rooster?"

Henry looked like he had been slapped a death blow. "Oh my, no. I'd have to trade for a lot of chickens for all those things."

"You get them cheap, Mr. Franklin. If you want to trade for my quality chickens, you'll have to trade fair. My chickens are the best in the county."

I glanced at our poor, hot chickens trying to cool themselves by flapping their wings in the dust under the trees. They didn't look like blue-ribbon winners to me.

But when Mother finally got through with Henry Franklin, he drove away with Cackle and two very light, non-laying hens. Mother had her large box of black pepper, a box of fine chocolate, all of those flavorings, a two-year subscription to the farm magazine—*and* the pretty picture for our wall. It must have taken Henry a long time to figure out a way to get that much out of those scraggly old chickens.

Dad was still chuckling as Mother said, "I think I'll make us some strawberry-flavored cookies for supper."

Dad laughed and said, "When the next salesman comes by, I want you to trade that old, poor, black horse for one of those fancy new farm tractors with all the equipment."

I smiled. Mother had really put one over on Henry Franklin. And when he had time to do some thinking, he would realize it. He would mark our farm in his little black book as a place to pass on by on his next selling spree.

Mother was a super chicken salesman. ❖

Changing Fortunes

By Lydia Mayfield

I was walking into town along the railroad track with five children, our three and my sister's two, whom we were keeping for the summer, or possibly for the duration. It was during the worst part of the Depression. My husband, who was busy cutting hay, suggested that I take the old Ford. There was at least half a tank of gas in the car, but where would we ever get the money for more? So I decided to walk. If we took the shortcut along the railroad track it was only five miles. We did a lot of walking during the Depression.

I was feeling very discouraged, desperately poor and hopeless. It was really a little thing that had gotten me into such low spirits, but it had seemed like a disaster that morning. I had at least a bushel of good green beans to can and plenty of jars, but not a lid in the house. Unfortunately, like all the other farmers, we already owed the grocer a big bill—and now he had gone on an all-cash basis.

My only hope was to try to trade him two dozen eggs to be delivered in a week or so for a box of lids. Eggs were 6 cents a dozen, and a box of lids cost 11 cents. Our hens were in a summer slump and were not laying well. I was sure he would refuse, but I still was determined to try. I needed to can those beans.

Really, we were very fortunate during the Depression compared with many city people. At least we had plenty to eat. We had our own meat, milk, butter, eggs and vegetables, and we even managed to trade our wheat for flour at a nearby mill.

But money was a very different story. A penny looked as big as a dollar—and we did not get our hands on many pennies. The purse I was carrying contained four pennies hoarded for stamps. It cost 2 cents to send a letter, and the post office always demanded cash.

The children ran on ahead. It was a lark for them to run along the tracks picking flowers and finding odd bits of rock and trash. I walked slowly behind them, feeling dismal and very sorry for myself. Then I noticed a small roll of dirty paper with a rubber band around it that the children had missed. When I unfolded it I could hardly believe my eyes. It was money—real money! Three one-dollar bills!

I felt as if I had come into a fortune. I rubbed off the dust and put the precious bills in my purse. Instead of feeling hopelessly poor, I was suddenly full of strength and hope.

I walked into that little grocery store with new courage and self-assurance. I had money enough to pay for a whole sackful of groceries, and I really splurged. I bought not one box of lids but a whole dozen, enough for canning all my beans as well as the apricots and peaches that would soon be ready. Besides that I bought a 5-pound sack of sugar, a canister of salt, and two real luxuries: a can of tobacco for my husband (who had been trying all kinds of substitutes, including corn silk), and the biggest luxury of all, a 10-cent sack of candy. You got a lot of candy for a dime back then. Best of all, even after my spending spree, I still had a whole $1.17 left in my purse!

After resting briefly in the town park, we walked back home, nibbling on the candy as we walked. I am sure the children got rather tired before we were home, but I didn't. That $3 had transformed me.

Things never seemed so hard after that day. Maybe economic conditions really improved a bit, or maybe it was the self-assurance and the new hope that little roll of dusty bills gave me. ❖

Depression Energy Crisis

By Virginia Petroplus Killough

Most of us remember the energy crisis of the 1980s, when motorists lined up in long queues to buy gas and many public buildings covered windows and turned down thermostats to conserve energy. But in a small, personal way, I had already been through an energy crisis once before. It happened to me, as it happened to many others, during my childhood back in the Depression.

One day the electric bill came. Mama, calmly ignoring it, went down to the basement and brought up an old kerosene lamp. What had been a sentiment-filled reminder of her early life in the country was about to be restored to a useful life.

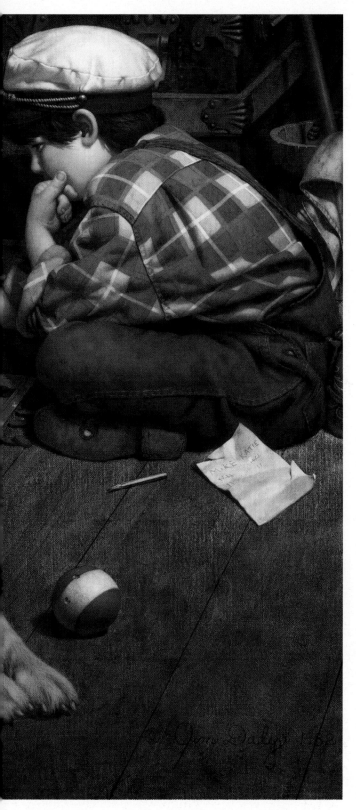

I was given a nickel and a quart milk bottle and instructions to buy 5 cents' worth of kerosene from the corner gas station. When the electricity was shut off a few days later, we were ready.

Of course we missed the radio, but there were always books from the library. Some of my happiest memories are of the six of us sitting around the kitchen table, reading or playing checkers or a quiet game of dominoes in the warm glow of that kerosene lamp.

Hot water? There was the teakettle. Baths? Saturday night only. Refrigeration? We didn't even have an icebox, so that was the least of our worries. Mama kept the milk and butter on the icy back porch all winter. In summer we bought only what we could use immediately.

Soon after this, the gas bill came. It, too, was an impossible hurdle. Daddy went out and brought home our stove for the duration—a long, three-burner kerosene model with a separate little tin oven to perch on top. At times this stove gave off a terrible odor, but it was a source of heat, and we had macaroni and lentils and homemade bread in winter, and in summer, green-bean stew from the garden. The cooking problem was solved.

For heat we still had the old coal furnace. We closed off three enclosed porches to conserve our small coal supply. That dwindling pile of coal must have been a nightmare to my father on cold January nights.

About this time, he acquired what I thought was a rather peculiar habit. He would put a bushel basket on my sister's wagon and walk down to a certain spot on a nearby railroad track where odd pieces of coal were sometimes scattered about. When he came home, the bushel basket was full of beautiful, hard, black, shiny coal, patiently gathered piece by piece. Even then it had a jewel-like quality to me—like black emeralds. That was how our father kept us warm.

Of course, we had long since put the car safely away in the garage. It had not been driven for months. Daddy put it up on blocks to save the tires and we walked. We were "in walking distance" of everything. We walked to school, to the park, to the forest preserve, to the library, to church. It was five miles to the zoo, five miles back. But we walked.

In particular, I remember spending that Thanksgiving with our dearest friends, who lived far, far on the other side of town. I remember the warm welcome, the laughter, the pumpkin pie Mama carried over, the feasting, and then the walk home, the six of us all together in the darkness, moving contentedly, quietly, through the soft flakes of the first snowfall of that enchanted year.

I suppose those simple ways of facing a crisis are beyond the reach of most of us these days. But once upon a time, that was the way it was. ❖

The Patriotic Goose

By Ben Townsend

During the Depression I got an after-school job at the Mound Valley, Kan., *Times-Journal,* a weekly newspaper. My first duties were sweeping the office and learning to be a printer's devil. I took my work seriously, and it wasn't long before I was left in charge of the office on Saturdays. My pay was $1.50 a week, which would buy a lot of three-for-a-dime hamburgers back then.

Saturdays were the most interesting days. That was the day when the publisher went out of town with his family and left me to handle the business, everything from taking news items over the hand-crank phone to collecting subscriptions.

Mound Valley was a farm town and on Saturdays it was jammed with farmers coming in to visit and shop. They had very little cash and usually paid their subscriptions by exchanging various items. Skeet George, the publisher, had told me, "Take anything that's eatable and give them a receipt for a year's paid-up subscription."

Before a month passed, I felt more as if I were operating a general store than a newspaper office. I took in several bushels of wheat, gunnysacks of field corn, fresh eggs and every sort of garden vegetable. I dutifully marked down whatever was brought in and filled out a receipt for the farmer.

Then one day, a farmer came in carrying a goose under his arm.

"I think my paper's expired," the farmer said. "I want to renew up."

I stared first at him, then at the goose. Up until now, I hadn't taken in anything that was *alive.* But I knew a goose was edible, so I figured it was a fair exchange, even though I didn't know where I was going to put it.

As it turned out, I never had any problem storing that ornery goose.

The farmer took the receipt, read it, then folded it and crammed it in the big pocket of his overalls. He handed the goose to me. A feeling of desperation gripped me as I stood there, holding the goose and watching the farmer go out the door.

I had no idea what I was going to do with it. But the goose made that decision for me. Without warning, he uncoiled his neck and, with a furious honk, clamped his bill onto a tender spot on my neck. I screamed and threw down the goose—which was exactly what it wanted me to do.

Flapping and honking, it half-flew, half-ran through the office and out the open back door. The last I saw of him that day he was scampering up the street toward the city hall.

I knew the publisher would be back shortly so I set out to balance the books. I had no intention of chasing the goose, and I wasn't going to tell the publisher it had gotten away, either. I removed two or three pears from each of several boxes that had been brought in that afternoon and put them in an empty box I dug up in the storeroom. Then I threw in a few ears of corn and marked the box down as the farmer's exchange for his subscription.

Little did I realize that that goose was destined to become the most famous goose in the town's history. Soon it was to become known from one end of town to the other as "the patriotic goose."

The creature had no difficulty surviving in Mound Valley. The town abounded with vacant lots, and every day it was seen foraging through them for food. Merchants soon adopted the goose. They set out galvanized tubs filled with fresh water for it to bathe in and drink. On the sidewalks in front of their stores, they scattered grain for it to feast on. It was soon fatter than most of the Depression-raised kids.

When fall came, school started. It was at that point that the goose began to make history.

The little school organized its first band, and every kid wanted to play in it. More than one family went on a steady diet of pan gravy and fried potatoes so their son or daughter could have a secondhand horn and play in the band.

As this was the town's first attempt at musical culture, there was some problem finding someone who could teach the children how to play their instruments. And when someone finally was located, it turned out that the only songs he knew were *The Star-Spangled Banner* and *America the Beautiful*. But the small band was the town's pride, and it was soon playing those two numbers at all civic events.

Then a strange thing happened. Wherever the band performed, the goose showed up. The patriotic music seemed to have an effect on it. The goose would waddle up behind the band director and stand perfectly motionless. Then, as the numbers were being played, it would stretch its neck and hold its head up proudly as if it understood the meanings of the songs.

As these numbers were rendered at every town function, it was not long before the goose was appearing at church gatherings, reunions, basketball games and the Saturday-afternoon band concert. In short, wherever the band played *The Star-Spangled Banner* and *America the Beautiful*, the goose was there.

The townspeople took to applauding the goose more than the band, especially when several months passed without the band adding any numbers to its repertoire. It wasn't that the kids hadn't made progress; the town just couldn't afford new sheet music.

In its second year accompanying the band, the patriotic goose of Mound Valley met with a traumatic experience.

Skeet George had published some nice editorials about the band. As a result, money was raised and sheet music for two or three additional numbers was purchased for the band. One of those was an inspiring march, the title of which now eludes me, and it was scheduled to be played for the first time at the opening basketball game.

The goose appeared and was given its usual applause as it stood at attention during *The Star-Spangled Banner*.

Then, upon finishing the anthem, the band immediately moved into the new march. With the first bar, the goose leaped in fright, its feathers ruffled. Frightened, it ran, slipping and sliding across the gymnasium floor, making its escape through the open door near the peanut stand.

After that, it avoided the band like the plague.

The patriotic goose continued to roam the town, feasting on the merchants' handouts, nesting in one of the vacant lots. Then, one day, it vanished. It was never seen again.

Farmers and townspeople talked about its disappearance for days. Many said it had died of fright after hearing the band's new number. "If the band had stuck to the old standbys, the goose'd still be around," they claimed.

Whenever my opinion was sought, I agreed that it had probably been frightened off by the new march. I wasn't about to tell them that I'd gotten awfully tired of pan gravy and fried potatoes so I could learn to play a cornet. And thus it had come to pass that one weekend during the Great Depression, I'd taken the goose home. For two days my family had the most sumptuous meals we'd enjoyed since they had begun scrimping on the grocery money in order to buy me a horn.

Needless to say, the main course was goose and potatoes—mashed, not fried. ❖

© *Wiped Out* by Jim Daly

Making Do, Doing Without

Chapter 2

I was puttering around in my side shed the other day when amazingly I came across a jar of marbles left over from my childhood. Probably the last time I had them out I was shooting for the prettiest agate in the ring. I was left-handed and looked so awkward that my foes often didn't mind playing "for keeps"—even for some of their favorite marbles—but I was a pretty good shooter.

Finding those marbles made me wonder why I am the kind of person who keeps virtually everything I've ever had—or at least everything that didn't completely rot or rust away.

I, like many of you, grew up in hard times. There is something about not having much that makes you hold onto what you do have, whether that is marbles or more practical things like screws and bolts.

I have every nail and board left over from the last renovation to the old family home. I have every extra screw, nut and bolt that has ever been included in packages of pantry shelves, pieces of office furniture or new tractor parts. Whenever I tuned up our now-antique pickup I always kept the old spark plugs and ignition points, figuring I might need a spare set along the road someday. Much of this now inhabits that side shed in our barn—a musty old place near and dear to my heart.

I have said that my side shed is the equivalent to Janice's button box, where she rummages for the perfect button or snap for her latest project. She, of course, points out that her button box fits neatly in a drawer in her sewing cabinet, while my side shed looks like … well, you get the picture.

One old proverb from the tough Good Old Days gone by was: "Use it up, wear it out, make it do, or do without!" Part of using it up was holding onto it until some useful purpose made itself known.

Janice and I have been blessed with having lived in the same place long enough to have plenty of places to putter, and plenty of "one man's junk" that is still our treasure. Those marbles, for instance. I know right where there is an old Ball canning jar that would look great filled with marbles and adorning that whatnot shelf I've been promising Janice I'd build her.

Of course, that means I'll have to build the shelf, but I think I know right where I can get the boards and wood screws for it.

It's a good thing I held onto all that junk. Otherwise today I'd be headed for the store a lot more often instead of making do or doing without. That's what I would have done back in the Good Old Days.

—Ken Tate

The Poorhouse

By Fay MacKenzie

As a child, I truly believed there was a place called "the poorhouse." It was located somewhere in northern Wisconsin where I lived.

Details were never supplied, but I assumed it was a large, dark, gloomy building with iron bars at the windows and surrounded by barren land. It would be desolate and cold. You would sleep on a bed of straw, and "they" wouldn't feed you. But if you were there, it would only be because you deserved it. The poorhouse was where you were certain to end up if you lived beyond your means.

"Do you want us all to have to go to the poorhouse?" my grandmother used to say. It wasn't a question; it was a statement, an answer to any silly request for an unnecessary item.

In the post-Depression days of the 1930s, living in the country, we knew no particular social class. We knew no one who had more than we did and we knew no one who had less. Neat rows of trees lined the rural roads. Their orderly line said they had been planted by the Civilian Conservation Corps, the C.C.C., as it was called. With men struggling to support their families, such programs were set up by President Franklin D. Roosevelt to help the working class regain some measure of financial security.

I was lucky. We lived in a nice log cabin built by my father, just a mile down the road from my grandmother's farm. My mother sewed my clothes, and my brother, Jack, and I shared a beautiful collie dog named Skippy. I was also the proud sole owner of a wooden bank shaped like a clock, and I allowed myself the extravagance of coveting nickels for it.

It apparently was my grandmother's duty to reinforce more conservative qualities in me. I once asked her, "Where is the poorhouse?"

"Over the hill," she said, and that was all there was to that. She refused to be drawn into an in-depth discussion of the matter.

Years later I heard her say, "I always kept a $100 bill in the sewing-machine drawer for emergencies." Whether this was a fact or not, I never knew. I never saw the bill, but I had no reason to doubt what she said. A sewing-machine salesman had swept the countryside with a surefire sales pitch, a demonstration of how the wonderful Singer treadle sewing machine could actually sew through a wet shingle. And so it did. I supposed if a $100 bill, or any other treasure for that matter, lurked in the farmhouse, the sewing-machine drawer would be the perfect place for it. Judicious planning and careful spending, however, were expected to prevent emergency situations.

Any desire for store-bought dresses and shoes was satisfied by daydreaming in a world of fantasy with the "wish book"—a catalog from Sears, Roebuck and Co. or Montgomery Ward (or, as we called them, Sears and Sawbuck and Monkey Ward). Those catalogs became worn and dog-eared in short order.

We did a great deal of shopping through mail order—not for frilly dresses or patent-leather shoes, but most likely for long winter underwear and warm snuggies.

I dreamed for a lot of things but dared not ask. The promise of the poorhouse was a powerful force.

When we moved into town, my spending habits underwent no severe change. I remained frugal. One Christmas I was given 50 cents for shopping and was allowed to go to the store by myself. There was a Big Little Book for 10 cents for Jack, and a lovely, genuine gold brooch for 15 cents for my mother. When I had finished my selections for all the family, I still clutched an Indian-head nickel. The poorhouse people would never see me!

I had never heard of anyone having or using charge accounts. The first time I went grocery shopping with my friend Weezie, she left the store with a sack of groceries without any money changing hands. It was difficult to control myself until the bell on the door clanged behind us.

"Weezie," I said quietly so the grocer wouldn't hear me, "you didn't pay him."

"Oh," she said lightly, "we don't pay here."

That was all she said. But I certainly knew where she and her family were going to have to go someday.

I drove past my grandmother's farm today, my purse full of charge cards, and in a car that won't be mine for a few more payments yet. Suddenly I missed the Good Old Days when we saved first, bought later. We took better care of our things then. After all, we counted our pennies and thought a long time before purchasing anything.

The farm is empty now and Grandma is gone, but her basic honest philosophy remains. "Do you want to go to the poorhouse?" It was not a threat. It was a reminder to live decently and realistically. Besides, there were some things more important than luxuries that no amount of money could buy. Wasn't the love we shared among our family the most valuable possession of all? ❖

Recycler Supreme

By Ann Baumgard

She lived long before the days of modern recycling—my ma, that is.

Only yesterday there was a quarter-page advertisement in the daily newspaper encouraging people to bring bundled newspapers, glass and flattened cans of all kinds to the recycling center rather than put such things on the curb for weekly trash pickup. "Help the economy—alleviate the waste problem—aid charities with recycling monies," the ad announced.

Ma didn't need to be reminded in her day. She had her own ideas of thrift, recycling and ecology. "A penny saved is a penny earned," she'd quote.

Newspapers? She had many uses for them. She laid sheets in traffic areas on the freshly scrubbed kitchen floor until it was perfectly dry. Then she'd pick the pieces up and lay them aside. Badly torn pieces were crumpled and used to buff newly blackened stoves or clean sooted-up lamp chimneys before they finally helped start the kitchen fire. Some sheets were used to cover kitchen cupboard shelves or line cupboard drawers. "Inky smell helps keep pesky ants away," she'd quip.

Papers wrapped packages and covered schoolbooks to keep them looking nice so they could be resold to kids in grades lower than my sister and me.

Ma would save bottles and broken glass and "worn-out" rags for the rag picker who came around twice a year. For her efforts she would get a few cents or some little trinket that could be used as a gift.

Tin tobacco and syrup pails were saved for kids' dinner buckets or for storage. Pa kept nails and screws and whatnot in a pail that he hung in the barn. Ma kept buttons and sewing supplies in another. We tied the pails around our waists when we went berry picking. My sister and I used them to carry cool drinks to men in the fields.

When a pail showed signs of rust or abuse it was delegated to the barn to be used as a measuring container for stock feed. None was thrown on the "hopeless heap" of rubbish until it had outlived any possibility of usefulness.

All year long Ma recycled the shells from the eggs she used in cooking and baking. She'd dry the shells in the warming oven of the big cookstove, then crush them and save them. Then, in winter, she would throw the bits and pieces into the straw that covered the henhouse floor. The hens kept busy scratching for the shell bits

Newspapers? She had many uses for them. She laid sheets in traffic areas on the freshly scrubbed kitchen floor until it was perfectly dry. Then she'd pick the pieces up and lay them aside.

Family Fun by the Stove by Charles Berger, House of White Birches nostalgia archives

that provided them with calcium for good egg production. "They've got to have lime for future eggs or else they'll satisfy their need by eating the eggs in the nest," Ma always said.

Ma recycled yarn, too. She'd unravel the good parts of worn-out, hand-knit mittens and stockings, wind the yarn in skeins and carefully "souse" them in warm, soapy water. Then she'd rinse them, squeeze them dry as best she could and hang them above the kitchen stove to straighten out so they could be reused. She had an uncanny knack for knitting short pieces of yarn together without ever tying a knot.

Grandma, who lived in town and did catering for wealthy summer resorters, garnered worn-out things from them and sent the "treasures" to Ma. Ma could do wonders with buttons, braid, trims and good parts of worn clothing. "A little soap and water and a little bit of know-how can do wonders," she'd declare.

Since I was the smaller of the two girls in our family, I inherited hand-me-downs. However, Ma could disguise "made-over" coats and dresses so well that I didn't mind. Gorgeous "jeweled" buttons added glamour. Silky braid covered worn hemlines. Soap and water helped, too. This made me happy—and Ma saved a pretty penny.

She saved store-bought underwear that was partly worn out, using good parts to repair holes in newer garments. Worn parts made excellent mop rags and stove buffers.

Carefully bleached flour sacks were made into under-bloomers for school wear. The sacks that didn't bleach out too well became dish towels; thus Ma saved us from the embarrassment of wearing undies bearing labels like "Gold Medal" and "Big Joe." The sacks also made pillowcases and tablecloths.

Whenever Ma made brand-new school dresses for us, she saved the scraps and made a crazy quilt. What fun we'd have as we identified as many pieces as we could, if and when a new quilt was placed on our bed.

Oh, yes, she was a string saver, too. Most of the string was salvaged from cloth sacks of flour, sugar, salt, animal feed and the like that were sewn together with store string. A ball of string had its place in a drawer of the kitchen cupboard. In the event someone forgot to replace the ball, they got a sharp reprimand from the person who next needed it. (Pa kept twine and very heavy cord in the barn.)

It is difficult for this younger generation to visualize Ma's thrift. With all the shopping centers conveniently accessible, how much simpler it is to buy new rather than recycle. I know; I lived—and am living—in both generations! ❖

When ever Ma made brand-new school dresses for us, she saved the scraps and made a crazy quilt.

Depression Days

By Myrtle I. Sawyer

In the early years of the Depression, my husband's contracting business began to dwindle and soon came to a stop altogether. We had to search for other means of making a livelihood. No jobs were available, but we owned a truck, and so one alternative was to haul coal from mines about 70 miles west of the town where we lived in southern Wyoming.

Most everyone used coal- and wood-burning stoves and furnaces almost exclusively for heating and cooking, and coal was the one economical commodity people used to survive.

The winters were long and hard, and the roads to the mine were narrow, often muddy and choked with snowdrifts. Many times when my husband started for a load of coal on what appeared to be a perfectly nice day, before he was halfway to his destination, a storm would sweep blinding snow and freezing cold across the plains, making it almost impossible to see the road ahead.

Vehicles had no heaters in those days, so we always bundled up as best we could before we set out on a journey that might take anywhere from a day to a week to complete.

Other truckers also hauled coal for a livelihood. On one occasion, seven trucks were stalled at the mine, unable to get out because of bad weather. The drivers, knowing they had to get home to their families, commandeered a little Model T Ford that happened to be available. All seven men piled into the tiny car and set out for home in a blinding snowstorm. The driver could not see beyond the radiator, so my husband lay out on the running board to guide him.

It was a long, hard, cold trip, but luckily the Ford did not stall or get stuck in a snowdrift. All the men arrived home safely in the middle of the night. They were cold, tired and hungry, but they thanked God for their safe return on a trip that could have ended in tragedy.

People faced this and many other trials and tribulations as the Depression dragged on. However, not many people were depressed or discouraged. As a matter of fact, the hard times drew them closer together, as each reached out to lend a hand in time of need.

I helped support a household by baking pies, cakes and cookies to sell to those who were fortunate enough to have steady jobs. Those people, in fact, were doing quite well because of the Depression, as prices hit rock bottom and they could buy indiscriminately.

Between my husband's coal hauling and my bakery sales, we managed household necessities. But very little was left for clothes and personal items. On one occasion I went to a rummage sale with $2 and was thrilled to bring home much-needed garments for each of the five members of our family.

Christmas was a crisis in those days. I could not bear to have my children wake on Christmas morning without at least one gift, so I saved pennies throughout the year, and as the holiday approached, I searched the stores for bargains. On the day before Christmas, the merchants marked down all the toys to half-price. Then I did my shopping, hoping the items I wanted would still be there on sale day.

One year I spied two beautiful dolls on display before the holidays. What a delight! They were still on the shelf at half-price the day before Christmas. My daughters' bright, shining eyes the next morning showed that that Christmas morning was one of the happiest of their lives. Years later, after my daughters were grown, thoughts of those dolls still brought special memories.

I do not remember looking forward to the end of the Depression. We thought of it as a way of life unlikely to change. We were surprised and delighted when the economy gradually improved and returned to normal. My husband's business began to flourish and, after a few years, it was even better than it had been before.

However, the Depression did teach us some valuable lessons. We never took anything for granted, and we learned never to be wasteful or discard useful things.

Because of those lean days, I became a compulsive saver. Now my children often ask why I save all the things I do. I answer: "What if we have another Depression?" ❖

Choir Boys by Frances Tipton-Hunter © 1938 SEPS: Licensed by Curtis Publishing

The Lady Made Christmas

By Rachel Stander Low

It is sad to be 12 years old and have your mother tell you there'll be no Christmas this year. There was a Depression, whatever that meant, and my papa was out of work. *All* the men in Coreyville were out of work. Soon there would be no money, and *then* what would we do? She said we wouldn't tell the four youngest children yet. That way their disappointment wouldn't last so long. Since I was almost grown-up, she knew I would understand.

I wanted to cry but I didn't. I just said, "I'm glad you told me," and went outdoors. That's the trouble with being 12 years old. You're expected to act like an adult when you feel like sitting on your mother's lap and crying. After I went to bed that night, I cried into my pillow. I couldn't help it. I didn't tell anyone, not even my best friend, Mary Edith.

There was something for each of us to do, either speak a piece or sing a song. We had a girls' quartet and a boys' quartet. The little kids sang together and the big kids sang together.

If you had lived in Coreyville, Pa., back then, you would have felt the way my mother felt. The crops had failed because of the drought, and the coal mines, where most of the men worked, were closed. There was no money, no work, no future. Even the school was in danger of closing the next semester.

To add to all this, it had rained for days and days. The skies were gray; the houses were gray; even the people looked gray as they walked listlessly downtown. All they could talk about was hard times.

There was one other problem people discussed—the "rowdies," as they called them. They were three young men in town who had nothing to do but make trouble. They were all cousins named Jones, and each carried a rifle. Every once in a while we'd hear three gunshots followed by a wild "Whoopee!" They never shot anyone, but they scared the little kids and stole their dinner buckets and things like that. Once they kidnapped little Teddy Calvert and kept him for several hours. He was not hurt, but his mother nearly went crazy. They disrupted our school programs and other kinds of gatherings. All the kids were afraid of them.

Much more interesting was "the Lady"—the village mystery. Who was she, and why was she in Coreyville? She had moved there in the early fall and rented a little house. No one knew what she did all day until one dark night, a couple of boys peeked in her window and saw her typing on a typewriter. We figured she might be writing a book.

Every day the Lady took a walk. She spoke to everyone she met, but most everyone just grunted and went on. The postmaster told us her name, but we couldn't remember it so we just referred to her as "the Lady," and after we began to talk to her, we simply called her "Lady."

Lady did one thing that always surprised us: She came to church. Our church was a shabby little building, gray like the rest of the town. One Sunday a month, a minister came to preach. But we went every week because it was something to do. We sang a few songs and somebody read a chapter from the Bible. Then we visited awhile.

Lady came every week, and some of the women began talking to her. She was nice, and pretty, too, with black hair and black eyes. Her clothes were lovely, all in bright colors. She even wore an orange coat, not a bit like the black and brown coats our mothers wore. Besides, she had a bright blue car, which started just as soon as she turned it on.

On the first Sunday of December she walked over to a little group of women who were gossiping together and asked, "Aren't we going to have a Christmas program?"

At first the women were stunned and couldn't speak. Then a kind of chorus of excuses broke out: "We ain't got anybody to do it." "We can't have Christmas this year." "I told my kids to forget Christmas." "The rowdies would spoil everything." "There ain't any money for a treat."

Did I see Lady's black eyes snap? I was sitting in the back seat, and I heard every word.

"Listen, friends, of *course* we can have a treat. How many of you raise popcorn?" Several hands were raised. "How many raise sugarcane?" More hands. "Can't you spare a little popcorn and a little sorghum and we can make popcorn balls?"

A single dissenting voice broke the magic spell: "I ain't got a recipe."

"I'll get a recipe from one of my friends," Lady continued as if there had been no interruption, "then they'll all be alike. I'm sure Granny Jenkins will let you make them at her house so the children won't smell the popcorn. And I'll furnish the wax paper to wrap them in."

She paused, then said, "If you like, I'll take charge of the program part." To a chorus of "Yes, yes!" she turned and clapped her hands. "Boys and girls," she announced, "be sure to come to the church on Wednesday after school to practice for the Christmas program."

The children clapped and two of the boys shouted, "*Whoopee!*" That made everyone laugh because it reminded them of the rowdies.

As the mothers walked home, they thought seriously about the rowdies. Would they spoil the program? Maybe it wouldn't be safe.

But the following Wednesday, we were all at the church. There was something for each of us to do, either speak a piece or sing a song. We had a girls' quartet and a boys' quartet. The little kids sang together and the big kids sang together. There were two dialogues (we called them "plays"), and we practiced carols that everyone would sing. Because I was one of the bigger kids, I got to read the shepherds' story from the Bible.

Our mothers kept their secret, but I knew when they made the popcorn balls. It was when my mother said in an offhanded way that she had been over to see Granny Jenkins. After it was all over, she told me how some of them had popped corn in big, black spiders while others cooked the syrup, and then they all shaped the balls and wrapped them in wax paper.

After that they decided it would be nice to clean the church. They got together one day and scrubbed the floor and the pews and washed the windows and blackened the stove. They didn't touch the organ because they said it wouldn't be used. I had to clap my hand over my mouth to keep from telling what *I* knew!

You see, mothers weren't the only ones with secrets to keep. We had two surprises. The big one was that Lady had cleaned up the organ and mended it, and now it made music. She was going to play it when we sang carols.

The other surprise was part of the program. The program was to close with a tableau of the Christmas story while we sang *Away in a Manger.* Our tableau would show Mary and Joseph and the Baby Jesus, the wise men and shepherds—*lots* of shepherds—and all the "strangers" in Bethlehem who wanted to see the baby. The important people would wear costumes. Joseph would wear Lady's gold bathrobe and carry a broomstick for a staff. Mary, lucky girl, would wear a long, blue, flowering dress with a white veil on her head.

We made a manger out of a box with legs. For the Baby Jesus, we were going to use the Fletcher baby. The Fletcher baby was a girl, and we thought it was kind of a joke on God, but Lady said God wouldn't care. After all, He made girl babies, too, didn't he?

It was the longest December I ever knew, but the 25th finally came. Even the calendar cooperated by bringing the holiday on Sunday—and the sun was shining!

By 3 o'clock the church was packed. It was shining clean. There were no decorations, but we didn't need any. Lady had brought over a gorgeous big poinsettia, which she had placed in front of the pulpit. Most of us had never seen one so large, and its glory filled our little sanctuary. Lady herself wore a pretty red dress. I loved to look at her.

But just as we were about to begin, in walked the three rowdies! There wasn't a vacant seat so they just stood at the back of the church like three sentinels, leaning on their guns. What might happen now?

However, the program went on as planned. The congregation gasped when Lady sat down at the organ and started to play *Joy to the World.* The other songs followed, and after each one, the audience clapped. The little kids were so cute and their mamas and papas looked so proud.

I didn't make a single mistake when I read the Bible story, but a funny thing happened. I had practiced just like the others and they had heard the shepherd story until they practically knew it by heart, so when I came to the angel chorus—you know, "Glory to God in the highest...."—without even thinking what they were doing, they all joined in! My mother said it was like an angel choir.

The tableau was best of all. The Fletcher baby made a perfect Baby Jesus. When Mary, in her blue robe, walked down the aisle and took her

from her mother's arms and laid her in the manger, I saw women wiping their eyes. The baby didn't cry or anything—just played with her toes.

And then, with the singing of *Away in a Manger,* the program was over. We kids all sat down on the floor.

Lady stepped down from the organ and stood in front of all those people. She thanked them for coming, she thanked the boys and girls for working so hard on the program, and she thanked the mothers for providing the treat. The little kids shrieked with joy because they hadn't heard about the treat.

Then, looking straight back at Hank Jones, one of the rowdies—the other two had sneaked out—she said, "Mr. Jones, will you please bring in the three cartons you'll find in the teacher's storeroom behind you?"

Mr. Jones! I'll bet nobody ever called Hank "Mister" before! Polite as could be, he said, "Yes, Ma'am!" And he did it! It took three trips.

By this time, the little kids were squealing with delight and bouncing up and down. Lady explained how the treats would be passed out, and soon every kid in Coreyville, even the babies, had a popcorn ball.

There was one left. Lady said, "Mr. Jones, you have been so kind helping us. Will you accept this popcorn ball and our best wishes for a Merry Christmas?" We held our breath lest he swear or something.

But he didn't swear. What do you think he said? Just like a gentleman, he said, "Yes, Ma'am. Thank you, Ma'am," and he walked out the door!

It was all over, but no one wanted to go home. The kids devoured every last kernel of the popcorn while the grown-ups talked. They even told jokes and laughed.

When darkness began to fall, we all started home. On the way, I heard my mother say to my papa, "After a day like this, one can almost believe that sometimes maybe we *can* have peace on earth, goodwill to men, and we owe it all to the Lady."

My mother was right: We owed it all to the Lady. I thought, *If I can grow into a person as nice as Lady, I don't mind being 12 years old for a little while.* ❖

© *To All a Good Night* by Jim Daly

A Christmas Miracle

By Pat Ziegler

These lines are written on a beautiful balmy day in May. The birds are singing and the air is heavy with the perfume of lilacs. To enjoy it to the fullest, we walked slowly down the beautiful, tree-lined streets of our village to the pretty little brick post office. At this time of year, very few letters await us there in our box.

After twirling the combination and opening the little door, we did find a magazine and a solitary letter. We dropped both into our little basket and leisurely made our way home, drinking in the beauty of this gorgeous day. Arriving home, we sat down at our desk, picked up the lone letter, noted the postmark, and looked for a moment at the tired handwriting on the envelope.

Opening it, we read:

"Dear friends,

"I have had a busy day. I've been housecleaning, and boy, am I tired! Supper is over; the dishes have been washed and put away. I should be on my way to bed, but I feel as though I must write to you. During the day, I came across three little boxes on a shelf in a clothes closet. Year after year I wonder why I should keep them, but I just can't bring myself to dispose of them.

"Today I stared at them as I held them in my hands. One by one, I raised the covers and tears rolled down my cheeks as I looked at the contents. I went over, sat on the edge of the bed, and the floodgates opened. I sat there and cried and cried. Wiping my face with a large, blue bandana handkerchief that I carry in the pocket of my apron when housecleaning, I looked at the boxes again and a strange feeling came over me. Here in my hands was living proof that our prayers are answered.

"Had I forgotten? Dear God, no! How could I ever forget those bitter, cruel days of the Depression? The very thought of those days makes me shudder, and goose pimples cover my body. Like a bolt out of the blue, it struck. People, going merrily along day after day, were face to face with disaster, almost overnight.

"Our three children were 8, 6 and 4 years of age; two boys and a girl. We were living in a rural area about 4 miles beyond the Detroit city limits. The office where my husband worked closed and he became unemployed. We were buying our home on land contract. Unable to keep up the payments, we lost it through foreclosure. We did not own an automobile in those days since we lived close to a streetcar line and were in walking distance to stores.

"My husband managed to find odd jobs, and with an income that varied from $8–$12 a week, we found a cottage in badly run-down condition that we were able to rent for $10 a month. An iron kitchen range and a Round Oak heater provided heat, using soft coal and cordwood for fuel.

"Indoor conveniences? None at all! A creaking old iron pump in the dooryard provided us with plenty of sparkling cold water, and down at the end of a long path stood the outhouse.

"Pioneer living? We had it, day after day! We scoured the fields for growing things that we could eat—dandelions, lambs-quarter and mustard leaves for greens; wild berries in the nearby woods and in fence rows; pears and apples, all wormy, in old, abandoned orchards. Our little garden and a few chickens produced vegetables and eggs, for which we were truly grateful.

"Money, oh how scarce. Times without number found us with but a dime or quarter in the house. How well I remember what a quarter would buy: a quart of milk, 5 cents; oatmeal, 5 cents a sack; one-quarter pound of butter, 8 cents; ground beef, 8 cents a pound—these are examples of prices in those days.

"One day our oldest son was sent to the store with the only money we had in the house, a quarter—and he lost it. A catastrophe! Pride kept many a deserving family from running to welfare in those days.

"Ours was a religious family who, for generations, had the strongest faith in prayer and firmly believed that 'the Lord will provide,' and He has never failed us.

"Christmas was coming. If ever the prospects of a bleak Christmas loomed, those were the years. Adults can face the realities of life as a rule. But how does one face an almost hopeless situation where there are little ones? By prayer, of course. Did not the Master say, 'Ask and you shall receive,' 'My grace is sufficient unto thee'? And so, in our daily prayers, we petitioned Him to assist us with this problem.

"Right after Thanksgiving that year, an advertisement appeared in the daily newspaper announcing a contest to be conducted by Crowley, Milner Co., a large Detroit department store. Scattered throughout their toy department were posters of the various toy manufacturers whose products were on display and for sale. On each poster were one or more misspelled words. An entry blank was provided to each contestant. On the form were spaces where the errors could be recorded.

"My husband and oldest son entered the contest and proceeded to try out their skill. Their entries were submitted and we awaited the results, confident that they had correctly identified the errors. The Lord works in mysterious ways His wonders to perform. We had faith in His help.

"One crisp December day, the postman brought a special-delivery letter to our door. With trembling hands, I opened the envelope. We had won a prize in that contest! However, the judges had mistaken our son's name for a girl's name!

"The prize? A $75 Madame Alexander doll, a gorgeous creation. *Now* what to do?

"We went to the store about a week before the prizes were to be awarded to the winners in the store auditorium. Miracle of miracles, the store management offered us a merchandise certificate in lieu of the beautiful doll. As a humorous touch to the award program, our son agreed to go to the platform when his name was called to accept the beautiful doll. Then Santa Claus would explain the error and present him with the substitute prize.

"My goodness! Try and imagine what joy was ours at a time like this, to have a merchandise certificate of that amount to spend for Christmas. There were shoes, new blouses, dresses, pants, underwear and plenty to get a good selection of games and toys, as well as candies and all that goes to make Christmas a wonderful occasion.

"Memories of that wonderful Christmas are mine tonight, as I write to you about three of the items, the boxes I held in my hands today: a jigsaw puzzle, a darling set of china doll dishes, and an assortment of games—checkers, lotto and dominoes. If you find stains on this paper, it's because I just can't hold back a few more tears.

"And tonight, dear friends, I'm offering those precious trinkets into your keeping—my memories of a Depression Christmas of long, long ago. God bless you, Joan M."

The three little soiled boxes, holding those toys that three children played with for hours and hours in those dark Depression days, are now preserved, thanks to Joan M. Between plastic covers in a notebook is her tear-stained letter, a testimonial of her faith in prayer. ❖

Lizzie Was a Lemon

By Edna C. Norrell

*I*t was 1926, three years before the big bust of the Great Depression. Jobs weren't plentiful but most folks were working and making a living. Uncle Bim Craddick had never leaned toward work very heavily, preferring to hunt and fish or visit his girlfriend, Miss Hattie Lumpkin.

However, when he went to town one day he happened to saunter by the only car sales lot in the county, and there sat the most beautiful car he had ever seen. It wasn't a new car—about a year old—but it seemed to have been manufactured just for Uncle Bim. Only one thing wrong: The salesman said a down payment would be required. Uncle Bim couldn't just drive it off on a promise to pay. That left only one thing to do: Get a job.

After several days of looking, he finally landed a job at the only industry in the community, a sawmill. He was put in the bullpen, just about the hardest work there—taking away strips and slabs of sawed lumber. Uncle Bim stuck it out, though. The wages left much to be desired, but at the end of the month he had the down payment for the car. To town he went and he came back driving it! He polished and shined that car 'til it looked like a mirror. In fact, I once saw Hattie fixing her hair while looking at her reflection in a fender!

The car broke down one day. All the neighbors gave advice. Some said it needed new spark plugs, some said a condenser, others said a new overhaul would work wonders. Every passerby had an opinion, but after it was all done, the car still wouldn't move. Uncle Bim was about ready to trade it for a mule. Then Caleb Abernathy came along, took a look, spat out a stream of brown tobacco juice and told Bim, "That motor is shot. What you need is a new motor."

"How much will a new motor cost?" Bim asked fearfully.

"Cost more'n the car did to start with!"

Bim ranted and raved for a week about how he had been gypped by that smooth-talking salesman. Still the car sat; it wouldn't even make a noise when he tried to start it. All the spark plugs were replaced, a new condenser was added, the fan belt removed and looked over and put back, even the tires were accused of doing something wrong.

Then Little Joe Anderson asked Uncle Bim when he had put gas in last. "Well, about a week ago, I think!" Using a stick as a measuring device, he tried in vain to find the gas in the tank. There was none. He rode a mule to the nearest filling station for a gallon of gas, poured it in the tank and the car started the first try!

Then the Great Depression hit, and it hit everybody hard. Bread lines grew, banks closed and bank officials even killed themselves. Folks became desperate. Uncle Bim lost his job and the sawmill went bust because nobody had any money to buy lumber.

Uncle Bim swapped the car for a mule. "That car couldn't plow a crop," he said. "And right now, a crop is more needed than a ride in a car."

And I really think it was! ❖

Prairie Gold

By J.B. Cearley

My family had gone to Post, Texas, that Saturday afternoon. We had sold our cream and eggs and purchased what few staple items of food we could on our meager Depression-days income. About 4 o'clock that late June afternoon, we started the 16-mile drive back to our home on the South Plains.

I looked sadly at my worn shoes. I had admired a beautiful new pair in a store that afternoon. But they cost $2.95—a mountain of money for a broke 14-year-old.

As we drove toward the Caprock I saw a small cloud in the distance. "I hope we get a rain," I said. It had been almost too dry to plant a crop that spring of 1932. Our cotton and grain were up and clean of weeds, but it was too dry for them to do well.

Dad glanced up and scanned the western skies. "That little cloud doesn't have enough moisture in it to wet a straw hat," he said. "I'd sure love to see a little rain, too."

A few moments later, Dad gave the old Model A more gas as we began to approach the steep hill of the Caprock. Dust swirled on the dirt highway behind the old Ford. The worn motor responded sluggishly on the incline.

Loaded with Mom, Dad and four kids, the car began to labor as we started up the main hill. Dad gave the motor full throttle and he had it up to 40 miles per hour. But the hill took its toll on the old car, and Dad had to shift to second gear when we were halfway up the bluff.

The motor sputtered and coughed, but we finally made it up the hill and the land leveled out for 90 miles to the west. The old car began running much better again after the hard pull. Deep, rich farmland spread across the plateau of the plains. When it rained, this land produced abundantly.

I glanced toward the west and saw a thin scattering of low clouds. We were still 12 miles from home, and I began to calculate whether the clouds were over our sandy-land farm. It looked like we might be getting a sprinkle.

Fifteen minutes later we were within 6 miles of home when we suddenly saw a rainbow forming in the sky. As we drove another mile, the rainbow became more intense. The color was magnificent, as rainbows are on the plains.

I followed the bow from its crest down to the place where it met ground. I felt sure that the bow touched down in a pasture across the road from our homestead. That thirsty, 30-acre mesquite pasture was one large prairie-dog town, covered with prairie-dog holes. My brothers and sisters had watched prairie dogs many times. We often chased them back across the road because Dad said they would ruin our farmland if we permitted them to dig holes in our fields.

Jim Daly
©
1988

Depression Disposition

By Berniece M. Vaughan

Recently I heard a strange story about an old gentleman who must have been of my vintage and lived during the Depression of the 1930s. When this old gentleman's wife died, he grieved sorrowfully. His children were concerned because his health was failing so rapidly.

Finally he was at death's door, and finding nothing physically wrong with him, his puzzled doctor posed a question: "John, what medications do you take?"

John said, "Just those pills on the shelf in the bathroom."

The doctor found there a cache of prescription medications, all of which had been issued to the dead wife. The doctor said, "John, those are Mary's pills."

"Yes, I know," said John, "but I didn't want them to go to waste."

I really know where that poor old fellow was coming from. That Depression certainly left its deep mark on young people who were growing up then, as I was. I, too, hate to waste anything, especially food!

I always save leftover food. Perhaps that's why my refrigerator is so crowded with bits and pieces of former meals that there's no room for fresh food.

Actually, I kind of enjoy dinners made up of several days' leftovers. Some of my meals are not too well balanced, however. I've found myself eating a dinner of leftover scalloped potatoes and leftover mashed potatoes and gravy. I always have a fresh green salad with that starchy, fatty duo. That sort of legitimizes the excess calories—in my mind, anyway—and makes me feel less guilty.

My farmer friends frequently bring me huge amounts of produce that they've raised. I've been known to eat zucchini squash until it's a wonder I didn't turn green!

Tomatoes? I've enough containers of them in my freezer to provide my family with soups and sauces for years. I just couldn't throw them out!

I have a problem with disposing of clothes, too. Recently, I decided to clean two long clothes closets in my bedroom. I took each item out and looked at it fondly, remembering when I had bought it and where I had worn it, and then hung it back up again. *Maybe I'll lose some weight and be able to wear that sometime,* I said to myself. Of course,

Was there a pot of gold in that prairie-dog town? I had often heard people say that there was always a pot of gold at the end of the rainbow—if you could only find it.

I recalled reading in my history book that when the early Spanish explorers had traveled north along the Caprock, they thought they saw golden buildings in the distance. That area lay in a canyon just east of the Caprock in what is now the area between Lubbock and Amarillo. But the castles of gold turned out to be clay and rock mounds of a yellowish color.

Our old Ford clattered on home and we encountered the distressing remains of our hope for rain. Not a drop had fallen on our dry land. There was very little rain during those Dust Bowl days.

When I got out of the car, I looked for a minute at the dog town. I didn't spot any gold bullion, but I did see a thousand prairie dogs. The rascals were prancing about or sitting on the small mounds around their holes, barking. They were like fat, overgrown squirrels with short tails, and they dug deep holes for homes. I had heard that they could dig down to water, but I never believed that story. The water table was 70 feet down.

That Sunday afternoon I picked up a copy of a farm magazine and walked out to the big porch in search of a cool spot. Again I began thinking about those beautiful shoes I had seen in Post. I was ashamed of my worn shoes, but how could I earn money for new ones? I didn't have a cent.

I sat down on the porch, hoping a little breeze would begin blowing. I alternated between looking at my ugly shoes and the farm magazine. After I had leafed through its pages and read two short articles, I began to scan the ads. Suddenly it hit me: "Wanted, prairie dogs." To my amazement, the advertisement informed me that a person in Illinois would pay $6 and freight to anyone who could send him four prairie dogs.

I wrote to the man and explained that there was a prairie-dog town across the road from our home and that I would be happy to ship him the dogs. I began to visualize myself with $6 and that wonderful pair of shoes. I might even buy some pants; after all, $6 was a whopping pile of cash!

After four days, I began rushing to the mailbox, hoping to receive good news. It arrived the sixth day after I had written. The man would be happy for me to ship him the prairie dogs.

Now to catch them! They were tricky, but my older brother and I had often caught one. The small ones made good pets. We would rapidly pour 10 gallons of water down a hole, causing the prairie dogs to rush out to escape.

Now I had to trap at least four young, healthy dogs. The man wanted one male and three females. That wouldn't be hard, with a thousand from which to pick.

After doing some thinking, I got an old chicken crate with small air holes so the dogs couldn't escape. I put some grass and weeds in the back of the crate and covered one end and a portion of the top. I knew that prairie dogs loved privacy and a place to hide. The weeds and grass also gave them food.

I went to the barn and got Dad's 5-gallon bucket and filled it with water at the stock tank. I carried it to the road, then another hundred yards into the prairie-dog town where I had seen several fine specimens. I set the bucket down and walked back to the house for a tub. I would need plenty of water.

After I had lugged 15 gallons to the hole, I carried the old crate to the dog mound. But how would I force them inside the crate? I used my ingenuity; I found some boards and made a chute so the dogs would rush out of their hole and into the crate through the chute.

When I was ready, I dashed the water down the hole as fast as I could. Then I stepped back and waited. A few moments later, I heard the noise of the dogs as they fought the water and rushed out to see what was wrong. They scurried right into my crate and settled into the grass and weeds to hide.

I slammed the door shut, not knowing how many dogs I had trapped. I felt sure that I had eight or 10. Visions of those pretty shoes filled my thoughts. What would I do with the extra money? What a thrill!

With the dogs safely in the crate, I set about thinking of a way to get them to the house. Finally I enticed my younger brother to help.

Then I set about making a shipping crate. I found lumber, a saw, a hammer and nails.

After laboring for two hours, I felt that I had built the ideal crate. It was about 18 inches square and 8 inches high. There was a door through which I could provide food and water. Food would not be a problem; I filled a small pan with maize grain and put it in the crate—plenty to last the dogs for a week. The trainmen would give the dogs water. I felt sure they would fare well on the trip.

I kept the animals in the old crate for the remainder of the week. My folks could only afford one trip to town, on Saturday. That morning, I began transferring the prairie dogs into the new shipping crate.

After I had selected two healthy, fat prairie dogs and put them into the crate, I slipped my hand inside the chicken crate again and felt in the weeds and grass for another dog.

Suddenly lightning struck my finger! The mother prairie dog clamped her sharp front teeth onto my finger, biting a hole right through it. I yanked her out and threw her onto the ground. She scurried away as I ran to put alcohol on my sore finger.

Not to be denied, I returned to the crate, got out two more dogs and placed them in my shipping crate. Then I let the three others loose and they fled back to the dog town.

That afternoon, I took my prairie dogs to the depot. The man there told me they would water them and that they should make the trip in two days. I was thrilled.

When I got to town, I hurried to the store to admire my beautiful shoes. Perhaps in a week I would be walking into that store to plunk down ready cash and wear those new shoes all over town. I would be one happy boy!

But lightning struck my balloon on Tuesday of the next week when a letter from the depot man at Post came in the mail. I read that my dogs had chewed a hole in the side of the shipping crate and had escaped Saturday night before the train arrived. The dogs were gone.

Dad then told me that he was sure I could not ship the dogs in a wooden crate. It would take a metal crate to ship such animals, and the cost of a metal crate was more than I would get for the prairie dogs.

Sadly I glanced across the road. I saw all those frisky prairie dogs scampering around in that pasture. But there would be no $6 for me, and no pretty new shoes.

Later that afternoon, an old Chevy rattled to a stop at our house. Mr. Roper got out, talked with Dad for a few minutes, then turned to me and my older brother. "Would you boys like to chop weeds in my cotton patch for a few days?" he asked. "I'll pay $1.25 for a full day of work."

My eyes lit up and I spoke up quickly. "You bet we would!"

Perhaps that rainbow had set in his cotton patch just north of the prairie-dog town. I would have my lovely shoes at last! ❖

When I Was a Kid

By Douglas L. Talsma

When I was a kid in Flint, Mich., in the late 1920s and early '30s, things were tough. There was never enough money for all the things that we really needed. My mom said I was harder on shoes than any kid she ever saw. My shoes always had worn spots across the toes because I spent so much time on my knees playing toy cars and airplanes. This, of course, was hard on the knees of my pants, too. There was usually a big square patch on each knee.

When my shoe got a hole, did it go to the repair shop? No! My folks went to the dime store and bought a repair kit with two rubber soles and a tube of some kind of cement. They glued one of the soles over the bottom of my shoe. But after a little while, the cement always worked loose and the rubber sole flapped with every step.

Sometimes my folks didn't even have enough money right then for a repair kit. Then I had to fold up a piece of newspaper and push it down into the offending shoe to try and save my sock for a little while. ❖

Depression Disposition

By Berniece M. Vaughan

Recently I heard a strange story about an old gentleman who must have been of my vintage and lived during the Depression of the 1930s. When this old gentleman's wife died, he grieved sorrowfully. His children were concerned because his health was failing so rapidly.

Finally he was at death's door, and finding nothing physically wrong with him, his puzzled doctor posed a question: "John, what medications do you take?"

John said, "Just those pills on the shelf in the bathroom."

The doctor found there a cache of prescription medications, all of which had been issued to the dead wife. The doctor said, "John, those are Mary's pills."

"Yes, I know," said John, "but I didn't want them to go to waste."

I really know where that poor old fellow was coming from. That Depression certainly left its deep mark on young people who were growing up then, as I was. I, too, hate to waste anything, especially food!

I always save leftover food. Perhaps that's why my refrigerator is so crowded with bits and pieces of former meals that there's no room for fresh food.

Actually, I kind of enjoy dinners made up of several days' leftovers. Some of my meals are not too well balanced, however. I've found myself eating a dinner of leftover scalloped potatoes and leftover mashed potatoes and gravy. I always have a fresh green salad with that starchy, fatty duo. That sort of legitimizes the excess calories—in my mind, anyway—and makes me feel less guilty.

My farmer friends frequently bring me huge amounts of produce that they've raised. I've been known to eat zucchini squash until it's a wonder I didn't turn green!

Tomatoes? I've enough containers of them in my freezer to provide my family with soups and sauces for years. I just couldn't throw them out!

I have a problem with disposing of clothes, too. Recently, I decided to clean two long clothes closets in my bedroom. I took each item out and looked at it fondly, remembering when I had bought it and where I had worn it, and then hung it back up again. *Maybe I'll lose some weight and be able to wear that sometime,* I said to myself. Of course,

The doctor found there a cache of prescription medications, all of which had been issued to the dead wife. The doctor said, "John, those are Mary's pills."

"Yes, I know," said John, "but I didn't want them to go to waste."

I'm ignoring the fact that I have more recently purchased clothes than I have places to wear them.

I also save scraps of paper to write notes on. And the last piece of a bar of soap goes into a jar. I plan to melt it down and make shampoo for the dog or something. I haven't really decided just how I'll use it, but, *It's good soap,* I tell myself.

I've saved jars of all sizes and shapes for years. Only a new program for recycling glass has saved me from having to park my car in the driveway to make room in my garage for those glass jars!

When I think of my struggle to get through college in the depths of that awful Depression, I'm amazed at my own fortitude and persistence. I had to walk 3 miles to school, and then climb two flights of steep, wooden steps to reach my classroom. That walk was enough to discourage most young people, and a lack of proper food and clothing compounded my difficulties. But even during Missouri's severest weather, I was in the science building by 7 a.m.

My mother's skill at reconstructing my cousin Esther's hand-me-downs helped, but warm coats, raincoats and shoes were not on her agenda. The colors and materials of Esther's dresses weren't always appropriate for college wear, but I wore them anyway. I remember one dress in particular—sheer black crepe with lace inserts in the sleeves and skirt. Pretty fancy gear for dissecting frogs and dogfish in the science lab!

I think of those days now and wonder what my fellow students, who lived on campus in snug dormitory rooms and ate hearty, well-balanced cafeteria meals, thought of the skinny, bedraggled little farm girl in their midst. They were always kind to me, though, and I made some lasting friends with whom I have kept in touch for many years. I made good grades, too. I must have seen that college degree as my way out of the life of hardship that my parents endured on the farm.

In spite of my ability to cope with adversity, something about those Depression years left me with an acute fear of poverty. When I received $80 per month for my first teaching job in a two-room school in Farley, Mo., I opened an account in the little bank there and socked away $10 from each paycheck. I remember having $80 in the bank one spring when my father asked if I would loan him money enough to buy seed corn. There went my carefully hoarded nest egg!

I've always urged my children and grandchildren to save money for a rainy day. They smile at me indulgently and then go on their merry ways. ❖

What's a Budget?

By Dorothy M. Rathborn

ack when my husband Nelson and I started our married life, the Depression was at its height and money was indeed a scarcity. The small amount that we gathered had to be very wisely used if we wanted to "keep our heads above water." Nobody talked of budgets in those days—it was more commonly referred to as "getting by."

There were no sums to put aside for emergencies or vacations (much as we would have liked the pleasure), but there was a place for every penny with nothing leftover for what was considered unessential. We just hoped and prayed that illness wouldn't strike and that there wouldn't be any job layoffs.

We made up our minds right from the start that we would manage on whatever we had and would never, *never*—except in dire circumstances—buy anything on credit. This we managed to do, but it was a very rocky road for us to travel.

What a wonderful feeling it was to drive by that lot and know that it was ours! At last we were property owners. It was a large, unattended piece of land covered with an assortment of tall, coarse grasses and weeds, but it was all ours.

For the first three years of our marriage, we lived with my folks, and our eldest child was born there. One day when our daughter was 2 years old, Nelson came home with the exciting news that he had run into someone who had told him about a piece of land that was for sale at a very reasonable price. It turned out to be property that belonged to the local school district, and the school officials didn't feel they needed it any more.

It was in a little community just a few miles away, so the location was excellent for us. If we could just get a piece of land and start building a house for ourselves! That was a dream we had cherished for a long time.

The "reasonable price" was $7, but it might just as well have been $700 as far as we were concerned. But not to be stumped, Nelson started his search for the money. By borrowing a dollar here and a dollar there, he was finally able to make the purchase. This was one time that he felt the need for borrowing money, and he paid it back very promptly.

What a wonderful feeling it was to drive by that lot and know that it was ours!

"No matter what we do, we must have water first," said Nelson. So as soon as he had the time and the equipment—a hammer, pipes and some boards—he went to work on a well.

Time was almost as hard to find as money in those days. There was no such thing as a 40-hour work week with paid holidays. Consequently, Nelson had very little time each evening to get a well started. On rare days off from work, he worked out at the lot all day long. Many times I went with him. I sat in the car, doing my sewing or mending as he worked.

Sometimes water can be reached just a few feet below the earth's surface, but in our case, it was very deep in the ground. Drilling for it was done by means of a tripod from which hung a heavy weight. This was pulled up and down steadily onto the pipe until water was reached. Eventually it appeared—delicious, cool, clear, pure water.

Now we could start thinking of building our home! The plans were very simple. We had no formal blueprints, just a rough sketch showing the size of the building and where the various rooms would be.

The first thing Nelson had to do was dig a foundation, all by hand, of course. After that, with the aid of a rented mixer, he was able to pour in the cement.

He had rebuilt an old car chassis into a trailer to use for transporting the supplies. Right from the beginning it proved its worth, for we had read in the paper where some used cement blocks were being offered for sale. They had to be hauled about 15 miles. We had decided to build our house out of cement blocks, thinking that not only would it be quicker and cheaper to build, but also that it would be much easier to heat in the winter.

Little by little the blocks were laid, windows put in and a roof constructed. We couldn't afford to hire anyone to put on a roof for us, so we ordered rolls of roofing from Sears and Roebuck and Nelson put them on himself. Ah, good old Sears and Roebuck—they were to be our chief source of supplies in the months and years ahead.

Eventually the shell of the house was completed and Nelson installed the electricity. We decided to move in at this point and do more work on the house as time and money allowed. There were no partitions, doors, finished floors, ceilings or kitchen cupboards, but this didn't dampen our spirits. We could hardly wait to live in our own home, be it ever so humble.

We were proud that we had water inside our house instead of a backyard pump like so many of our neighbors had. Nelson had planned it that way, building the house around the well so that our source of water was inside when everything was finished. We did have to use a little hand pump, but that was almost fun, and we did have a sink to go with it.

For the first two or three weeks in our new home, there was no door on the bathroom—we just didn't have the money to buy one—and so we tacked up a heavy blanket in its place. A person soon developed a cough or a good singing voice while using the facilities! As soon as possible, Nelson bought a large sheet of plywood. We used it for a door until we could afford the purchase of a real one.

It was very hard to keep the house clean, for it had none of the advantages of today's automatic heat and labor-saving devices. An old iron stove furnished heat by burning up in very quick fashion the coal that we constantly fed into it. It scattered coal dust all over the place when we fed it and cleaned it out; you can imagine how a layer of dust was always over everything.

Our home was furnished "a la pick-up"— that is, with anything we could gather from relatives and friends. Their castoffs became our treasures. We borrowed a kitchen table and chairs from one of my aunts, and I always took such pride in using my pretty tablecloths and dishes on it. Oh, yes, I did have a good supply of linens, for in those days everybody did a lot of sewing and embroidery, which always made beautiful gifts.

Another aunt gave us a chair for the living room, and we bought a davenport and a chair at a very reasonable price from a friend. I also had a big upright piano; it took up a good deal of the living room, but it was my pride and joy. Our radio stood on an orange crate that I covered with a pretty curtain—and we made good use of the storage space inside the box.

Orange crates were used in many ways in those days. Two of them joined with a piece of plywood nailed across the top could substitute as a dressing table or desk. We put another one in the utility room to hold soap powders and cleaning supplies.

And so we went, me putting the feminine touches here and there, and Nelson concentrating on what could be done next in finishing the house.

I had a wash day, mending day, cleaning day, baking day, and many other days of specific duties. I hated wash day. We had no running hot water at that time so I had to heat up a supply before starting the washing. But we didn't want the expense of using the cooking stove to heat

Pages 56 & 57, © *The Ice Man* by Jim Daly

the water when there was heat from the heating stove that could be put to use. So, the night before wash day, before we went to bed, we would put a washtub on top of the heating stove and fill it with water, a pail at a time. We would put a lid on it, and by the time I got up the next morning, the water would be nice and hot.

It was hot all right, but it really wasn't nice. Remember the hard water that I mentioned earlier? Well, that water was so hard that a thick coating of red rust covered the entire area. It had to be scraped off carefully before the water could be used; otherwise the clothes would be badly stained.

We used an icebox for storing food in those days. Not many people could afford an electric refrigerator. In the top part of it was a deep section that was used to store the ice. It could be bought in 25-, 50-, 75- and 100-pound cakes. The usual method of obtaining it was to put a sign in the window telling how much you needed. A card for that purpose had different numbers for the different amounts printed along the edges; you just set the card in your window with the correct number turned to the top. The iceman could tell at a glance what you wanted, and he headed right to your door with your order.

This was quite a satisfactory way of keeping food fresh unless you let too much time pass before replenishing your supply of ice. As the ice melted, the water ran down a pipe into a basin under the box. If you neglected to check it every day, the water would overflow and go all over the floor. Nelson, however, soon devised a system that freed us from having to check the water level. He extended the pipe through a hole in the floor so the water ran right down to the ground outside.

We practiced "making do" economy just about every minute of every day. Unneeded lights were turned off and every morsel of food was put to good use. I always had a few leftovers that blended wonderfully into casserole dishes. Once a week I would gather all the little dishes of leftover vegetables that had accumulated and would combine them into a creamed dish. My children loved it! I think they were nearly grown before they realized that I was just using what was available instead of following a special recipe.

Each payday usually meant that another supply of nails or other building supplies could be bought, and each payday Nelson would study our finances thoroughly—very thoroughly. Anything leftover after all the necessities were taken care of was always wisely spent.

We allowed ourselves $5 a week for groceries and found that we could manage on this by being very careful. Small as it may seem now, this amount provided an ample assortment of meat, in fact, a much better variety than we can find nowadays. Skimmed milk could be bought cheaper by the gallon at the local dairy if we took our own container. We bought butter only for special occasions, and then I usually bought only half a pound.

Oleo was our chief margarine spread then. It was not packaged as nicely as it is now, and it always looked like a bar of lard, for it was against the law to color it for the consumer at that time. A little package of coloring was included with each package. If you remembered to let the oleo reach room temperature first, it wasn't too difficult to mix in the coloring. But if you forgot, it was almost impossible to blend it thoroughly and there would be orange and red streaks throughout the mixture.

Once in a while the grocery stores would offer "specials." Many a time I bought 3 pounds of hamburger for a quarter or, better yet, five delicious pork chops for only a quarter! Sometimes I would just buy a dime's worth of hamburger to mix with macaroni or rice.

The only allowance I had for myself was any amount leftover from the weekly grocery money. It was a small sum indeed, but it enabled me to have a little pocket money to do with as I wished.

No article of clothing was ever thrown away. Everyone passed things around in those days, for there was always someone who could use them. If garments could not be altered into something for another child, smaller articles were fashioned out of the material—pot holders, bibs, aprons and other such items. Buttons were cut off and saved. I accumulated a delightful assortment of buttons in a tin box; and the children always enjoyed playing with them.

Dressmaking and alterations were my specialty. It was always a pleasure and a challenge to see what I could do with the clothing that was passed around. Hems could be let down and decorated with lace or rickrack to conceal the original hemline. Darning and mending were regular tasks of housewives at that time. We even darned our nylon stockings in those days, taking care to wear the mended portions on the inside of our legs so that they were less noticeable.

After-Christmas sales were always a source of delight for me, as I usually found a few inexpensive items that could be put to good use. One time I bought a three-piece canister set for only 25 cents. They were a bit scratched, but that didn't bother me. I gave all the cans a fresh coat of paint and decorated them with decals, making them into a very attractive display for the kitchen.

It amazed me how Nelson could build a house like he did with no experience, very few tools and hardly any money. Occasionally there were a few mishaps, but that was understandable, considering.

The one thing that did irritate both of us was the front door. It faced west, which meant that it took all the brunt of the bad weather. During a heavy storm, rain always leaked through. We had to take action immediately, moving the furniture and turning back the carpet to keep things dry. Otherwise it sometimes took days for everything to dry out.

Our entertainment in those lean days of the Depression was mostly of the home-oriented variety. We did manage to get to the movies once a week, as the price of admission was much more in tune with a person's pocketbook than it is now.

Television hadn't arrived in our lives, but radio played a significant part in it. Every day while working on my household tasks, I would listen to my favorite programs, such as *Our Gal Sunday, Ma Perkins, Clara, Lu 'n' Em, Myrt 'n' Marge* and other such stories dealing with the simplified lives of those times. And in the evening, we all enjoyed listening to *Amos 'n' Andy, The Lux Radio Theater, Grand Central Station, Edgar Bergen and Charlie McCarthy* and many other stories and features dealing with romance and mystery.

There were programs for the children, too, in the early morning and late afternoon. Our daughter loved to listen to *The Singing Lady* and *Uncle Neil,* who always chanted the same ditty each day:

"Stop, look and listen
Before you cross the street;
Use your eyes, use your ears,
And then use your feet!"
Orphan Annie was another of the children's favorite programs.

Radio didn't interfere or slow you down at whatever you were doing. There was no picture to distract you from your duties.

The rest of our entertainment was either in our homes or in the churches and schools. We women held luncheons with moderately priced but delicious food. The menus we planned with such limited funds as we had might surprise you.

After enjoying our meal, we would all work together to clean things up, sending the children out to play. Then we spent the afternoon in delightful chatter while we worked on our handiwork. I never knew a woman who didn't sew, knit or crochet in those days.

What I enjoyed most, though, were the potluck suppers that we had in each others' homes. All the family were included and there was always a delicious assortment of food with each person bringing her specialty.

We didn't need much excuse for a party. Birthdays were always celebrated, as were graduations, Christmas and other holidays. Sometimes we played cards or games. But I liked the singsongs best, with a group of us gathered around the piano, singing all the old favorites and some of the new songs. My cousin and I took turns playing the piano and I always liked to do this; it was a delight to accompany such a peppy group. Sometimes a few couples would dance.

And so life went on. With a little ingenuity and ambition, we were able to acquire furnishings and fixtures for our home, making it a comfortable and cozy place in which to live.

After the Depression finally ended, prosperity came creeping in. We sold our little house and moved to town, into a much bigger and nicer place. But there was a sad feeling in our hearts as we left the first house we had shared as a family. There was so much of us in that little home—our dreams, our happy times, and, of course, a few of those hard, depressing times that come to everyone at one time or another. But our life together in our little home was an experience that we shall never forget. ❖

© *Our Daily Bread* by John Sloane

Loving Neighbors

Chapter 3

I don't know how many times I asked myself, *Where would we have been without Ben?* Ben Littleton was our neighbor many, many years, and if it hadn't been for the help of the Littleton family, I don't know if the tough times would have been bearable.

It didn't matter if it was seeding time, plowing time or harvest time, our families shared strong backs, sweaty arms and helping hands on the steep slopes of those Ozark Mountains we called home. Ben was always grateful for our help, as little as it seemed to be, but I still don't know where we would have been without Ben.

There wasn't much around the farm Ben didn't know. He could shoe a horse, and gentle it, too. He could help birth a heifer's first calf, and could doctor them both if necessary. He knew every old-time cure and home remedy when the doctor was miles away and there was no money for the visit. And if Ben didn't know it, he could probably tall-tale you into thinking he knew it anyway.

That was our favorite leisure pastime—telling tall tales. In the winter, when harvest was past, we took time to spin our yarns in front of first his wood heater and then mine. When Ben and I got together the fish we caught grew longer and the deer we hunted were bigger.

My favorite times were after long summer mornings in the fields when we relaxed in the shade of a spreading oak. Wives and daughters brought victuals with pitchers of lemonade to drink, we said grace and then broke bread together. Maybe it was too hot to go inside, or maybe we just liked the perfect parlor provided by God outside, but there we shared our words and friendship as freely as we shared our labor.

The Good Book says that the second greatest commandment is to love your neighbor as yourself. Well, I reckon that no neighbor obeyed that commandment any better than Ben Littleton, unless it was his children, who learned it from him.

I lost my good friend Ben a few years ago. He was 90. The last time I saw him in a field was about three months before his death, and he was sitting on his old Ford tractor, raking hay for a neighbor.

Where would we have been without Ben? Like so many others who share their memories in this chapter, we would have had even tougher times without the blessing of sharing loads between loving neighbors. We were poor enough as it was. Without Ben we would have been all the poorer.

—*Ken Tate*

Hobo With Pockets

By Lorene Mutti Clark

My most vivid childhood memories are those set in what is now called the Great Depression: I simply remember those days as hard times.

Thousands of men who were unable to find work took to the road. Most of those whose paths led them anywhere near Bremen, Ind., knocked at our door—or so it seemed. Mother never turned one of these travelers away. If Dad wasn't home, she had them sit on the back steps while she prepared food for them. If my sister or I were home, she gave us the task of taking the plate of hot food to our waiting visitor. We didn't mind one bit—these men, Dad told us, were just poor men "down on their luck," victims of the times. They deserved our respect and help. After all, isn't that what we were taught in Sunday school?

If Dad was home when a "poor, wayfaring stranger" appeared at our door with a request for food, he was asked to step inside and be seated at the kitchen table. Dad sat there and visited with him as he ate.

One late autumn day, when a sharpness in the air signaled the approach of winter, an unforgettable, uninvited guest crossed our path. Tall and thin, he wore a long, burdensome-looking overcoat that almost touched his ankles.

Dad and he talked enjoyably together. This man spoke intelligently of world affairs and was knowledgeable on a variety of subjects. Before he departed, under my father's genuine, friendly interest, he took off his overcoat, turned it inside out and showed Dad his portable "carry-all."

A special inner lining had been sturdily sewn into his heavy wool coat and then divided into large pockets. Each pocket was for a designated item. Nothing had been overlooked. One pocket was for newspapers, another for sandwiches, another for old clothes. That imaginative fellow had made a pocket for any item that might be given to him. He did not intend to waste a thing.

If I live to be 100 years old, time will never erase from my mind's eye that scene of long ago: The unknown traveler spreading his weighty coat on our old kitchen table, and Dad gazing down at it as he listened to the visitor explain its contents.

Not everyone was as compassionate to these uprooted men as my parents were. One woman on our street told how she was asked for some bacon and eggs. Her reply was, "My good man, I can't afford bacon and eggs myself." This woman was in a far better financial state than our family, but the size of one's pocketbook does not determine the size of one's heart, and at no time was this proved true more than during the 1930s.

Our house was no doubt marked during the Depression days, for hobo signs do exist. Their origin came about when some vagabonds, eating a pot of mulligan stew in a freight yard, put together a set of signs to give clues on their surroundings to their fellow hobos who might pass through the area later.

Some hobo signs are illustrated below.

Today's hobo is a different breed from those men who stopped at our door in the 1930s. ❖

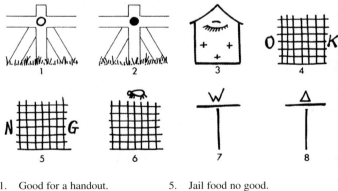

1. Good for a handout.
2. Cranky woman or bad dog.
3. Jail good for night's lodging.
4. Clean jail.
5. Jail food no good.
6. Cooties in jail.
7. Jail has rock pile.
8. Jail is a workhouse.

© *Wet and Tired* by Jim Daly

The Bank Closing

By Kenneth Haun

I slipped through the front door that Friday afternoon, seconds before the bank closed. It was an exciting day for me. I had received my first paycheck as a high-school principal and was anxious to open my first checking account.

Looking back on that memorable day in 1931, I remember that going to open an account was a pleasant dream coming true. One hundred and fifty dollars for my first month seemed substantial, a solid beginning for a new principal and his wife of two months.

Inside the door, I paused and looked around. I watched an employee, his eye on the clock, wait for the second hand to complete a final sweep before he closed and locked the door.

I was the only customer. The bank was small, much smaller than the more pretentious one on the other side of the street, and even though opening a bank account was new to me, I felt totally at ease in the lobby.

The cashier was behind the center window. He stood facing the side of his teller's cage, apparently unaware I had entered. I didn't know him although I had noticed him before when looking in the lobby on other trips to town.

Approaching, I could see he wasn't working but simply standing there, his balding head downturned and motionless. He seemed lost in serious and absorbing thoughts that required his total attention. He was a tall man, shoulders rounded under his dark coat, lean of build, serious and thoughtful, as I believed a banker should be, an elderly man in my younger eyes. I felt I was right in coming here and that this was the bank for me.

I waited. He returned to the present and saw me standing there.

"I want to open a checking account," I said. "I'm the new principal at Pruntytown School."

He glanced at the clock on the wall, now past the official closing time. He appeared to hesitate, as though uncertain about completing a transaction after closing hours, then reached under the counter for a printed form. I answered his questions. He handed me a checkbook.

"Good night," he said as I turned to go. His voice was pitched so low that I almost failed to understand his words.

While waiting for the door to be unlocked, I was aware he was watching me. He wasn't smiling but appeared austere, even

> *I stood for a moment before going on.*
>
> *I knocked. Footsteps approached from inside the house. The door opened.*
>
> *It was the bank cashier— the man who had taken my money.*

unfriendly. Suddenly I felt uneasy. Surely my late arrival wasn't the reason for his hostility. There must be something I didn't understand. I welcomed the opening door.

I had wanted to complete my banking before we drove to visit my wife's family over the weekend. Our few dollars in cash would buy gasoline and meet emergencies that might arise, and it was a happy feeling as we drove, believing our money was safe and knowing we could write checks to pay the bills coming due.

I was vaguely aware that banks were failing in those days, but they were impersonal failures, far away in other towns. I couldn't imagine, as we traveled, that I had been the final customer my bank would have. It was unthinkable that on Monday morning the door would remain closed and never open for normal business again, that my bank would be a statistic in a list of failures that marked those dark days of the 1929 Depression.

Teaching positions were hard to come by in those days and few candidates were chosen. I was fortunate, although the nature of my position fully occupied every minute of my working day. I was the only teacher for the 32 freshmen and sophomores enrolled.

We had finished the fourth of 10 daily high-school subjects we covered when I looked out the window and saw my wife hurrying up the steps toward the school.

I met her at the door. I could see she was troubled, almost ready to cry.

"What's wrong?"

"The bank," she said. "It failed. Our money's gone."

At first I rejected the shocking news as unfounded rumor, impossible, but by late afternoon everyone in town knew the story was true.

There was gloom that evening and bitterness toward the cashier who took my money. The injustice—even *dishonesty*—of accepting my money after banking hours,

undoubtedly knowing failure was coming, surely aware my money was the last the bank would ever accept, was beyond my understanding and forgiveness.

The two weeks after "the morning of the closing" passed, and the gloominess and bitterness faded into the background of daily happenings. The landlady sympathized with us. The farmer who brought our milk seemed unconcerned about the unpaid bill. Our Majestic radio payment, our first and only major purchase, required $5 of our cash-in-hand to meet the bill. Our cold, second-hand Chevrolet stayed parked a little more, but we managed to visit my parents one weekend and return to my wife's parents the next. On both visits, vegetables from their summer gardens found their way into our car. The shock of our loss receded.

Then, one Monday evening, with dusk fast approaching, I answered the telephone.

"Mr. Haun?" a voice asked.

"Yes, sir," I answered.

"It's important that I see you. Please come by my house at 9 tonight. I know it's late, but I'll leave the porch light on. I live up the avenue beside the river. Please come alone and don't mention to anyone that you are coming. My house number is on the mailbox by the curb."

Many banks closed during the Great Depression including the Peoples State Bank, Berne, Ind., shown here.
Photo courtesy of Rod Lautzenheiser.

I wrote down the number and said I'd be there.

"Who was that?" my wife asked, calling from the kitchen across the hall.

"Some man. He didn't say who he was. He wants to see me tonight."

I tried to explain why I was going, but she wasn't happy with my reasoning. I should have asked his name and what he wanted; why didn't I find out before saying I'd come? Going to a strange neighborhood in the dark to meet a man I didn't know could be dangerous. Anything could happen.

I failed to provide a convincing and reassuring answer. My assumption that some school-related problem was involved didn't convince her. I'm sure my youth and inexperience influenced my unhesitating agreement to be there. It seemed logical and direct to me.

If I went, she would go too, though after much discussion she agreed to wait for me in the car.

It was almost 9 when we turned up the avenue along the river. Occasional lights reflected on the moving water. Beyond the river we saw portions of the railroad yards and heard the clash of connecting couplings as the yard engine gathered a string of cars for travel the following day. Main Street was over there on the other side of the river.

We drove along until we saw the mailbox. Pulling to the side of the street, we parked beneath a streetlight near the steps mounting the slope toward a light visible in the distance.

The area was deserted. I left the car, making sure the doors were locked, and walked up the steps toward the light. My wife watched me disappear into the darkness. Realizing she thought I shouldn't go, her fear of something happening made me uneasy; it was an eerie feeling as I moved toward the dimly shadowed porch.

I stood for a moment before going on. In front of a window to the left, a swing hung, suspended by chains fastened to the ceiling. There was nothing more that I could see as I approached the door.

I knocked. Footsteps approached from inside the house. The door opened.

It was the bank cashier—the man who had taken my money.

"Come in, please," he said. "I wanted to call you sooner, but I had to be sure you didn't write a check. The record reflected that your paycheck was cashed. I held the money. It's here."

He gave me an envelope he had been holding.

"I hope," he said, "that you don't mention this to anyone. It could cause me embarrassment. But I wouldn't open your account unless forced to do so."

I took the envelope, stammered my thanks and left. I may have heard his name at a later time, but I don't remember it.

He's gone now, I'm sure, but my attitude toward bankers has been trusting and positive since that evening long ago, when I walked down the steps to my waiting wife with the envelope holding my money held tightly in my hand. ❖

The interior of the Peoples State Bank, Berne, Ind., shown here. The roll-top desk shown here is still in use by the owner of this photograph, Rod Lautzenheiser.

Christmas Giant

By Bertha Lazenby Knox

I was born in the early 1930s when our country was struggling to overcome the Great Depression. Just having enough food and clothing was a blessing. Often, as Papa thanked God for our meal, tears ran down his face. Papa wished he had more material things for his family. But no matter how meager our table was, we always shared with someone less fortunate.

One afternoon a few weeks before Christmas, there was a knock at the door. I opened it, and there stood the largest man I had ever seen.

A few nights before, Mama had read us a story about a giant who captured people to be his slaves. When I looked at the man, I thought the giant had come for us, and I was afraid.

Papa came to the door and talked briefly with the giant. Then Papa asked me to tell Mama to fix the man a plate of food. The giant was invited in to sit by the fire, for it was bitter cold. When Mama brought in the plate of food, I expected the giant to grab it and gobble like the giant in the story. Instead, he took the plate gently and ate slowly, enjoying every bite.

When the giant finished his supper, Papa lit the lantern and led the stranger to the barn to sleep. I didn't sleep too well that night, thinking the giant would break down the door and capture us.

Plans had been made to kill hogs the next day. Everyone was up at dawn, even the giant. Hog-killing time was a busy time and I usually was in the way. That particular day I stayed in the house, away from the giant.

The giant slept in our barn and worked on nearby farms. I think he knew I was afraid of him because he often offered to help me with my chores. It was my job to carry in the wood for the cookstove. One evening as I was gathering it, the giant offered to carry the wood for me. But I threw it down, ran into the house and slammed the door. He never offered to help me again.

There were no supermarkets in those days, but the rolling store came by every Saturday. Mr. Leonard would let me look around while Mama traded eggs for the things we needed. In a box was the most beautiful doll I had ever seen. The doll's face was painted to perfection and her dress was green satin. I held the doll gently, closed my eyes and wished Santa would bring me one just like it.

Later I asked Mama if Santa Claus would bring me a doll like the one in the store. She said, "I don't think so; it looks too expensive."

On Sunday afternoon a week before Christmas, our family went to the woods to look for a tree. Papa asked the giant to go with us. After the tree was selected, the giant cut it down and carried it home. He watched while we decorated it.

That night as we sat around the fire, Mama popped popcorn for us to make a rope for our Christmas tree. We cut out paper lanterns and a star for the treetop.

The next Saturday when the rolling store came by, the doll was gone. When I asked Mr. Leonard about it, he said that a man had bought it. With the doll gone it wasn't fun looking anymore.

That night we each wrote our name on a box and put it under the tree for Santa to put our gifts in. We knew there wouldn't be much, but we would enjoy whatever it was. Usually we received one gift along with apples, oranges and candy.

The next morning I rushed to the tree. In my box was something wrapped in brown paper. I couldn't believe my eyes—it was the beautiful doll!

The giant was gone that morning and we never heard from him again. It wasn't until many years later that Mama told me the giant had bought the doll for me. I don't know your name but, Mr. Giant, I want to say thank you for my doll. It made that Christmas one of the best Christmases I ever had. Thank you for being my Christmas Giant. ❖

The Goody Box Christmas

By Faye B. Gardner

*I*t was Christmastime during the beginning years of the Great Depression in a little valley town nestled in the Wasatch Mountains. In this little town lived a small family consisting of a daughter, two sons and their parents. They loved each other and seemed so happy. The parents enjoyed having the children's friends come to share dinner, parties, picnics, or just to play in the big yard beside the modest home.

This particular Christmas, however, the atmosphere seemed a bit different in the home and in the town. Missing was the gaiety that usually accompanied the Christmas-shopping season. There was less caroling, and the older people went about with somber looks on their faces. Not much was said about Christmas at all. The Depression had come to the little town and many people were not only out of work, but out of money and food as well.

The father of the little family had lost his job a few weeks earlier. There were no other jobs to be found and money was very scarce. As Christmas approached, both he and the mother seemed preoccupied and quieter than usual. But the daughter, who was quite a bit older than her brothers, wasn't worried. She knew everything would be all right for their Christmas; it always was. She looked at the many lovely things in the store windows and thought of dozens of items she would like to have.

On the afternoon of Christmas Eve, the father brought home a much smaller Christmas tree than usual and put it in its stand. After supper, the family gathered around the tree and each one got to hang his favorite ornament. The candles were placed in their little holders, which clipped onto the branches. Then the father lit each candle as everyone watched with bated breath. The tree seemed beautifully alive with light.

After the candles were lit, the little family listened to the mother read the Christmas story from the Bible. Then they sang some songs, said their prayers and tumbled into bed. The children were awakened every hour by the striking of the clock. They lay in bed, wondering if they dared ask if it was time to get up.

Mother had prepared her best dishes and soon had everything ready. Father loaded the car with mysterious boxes and they set out for Grandma's house only a few blocks away.

Christmas Greetings by Jay Killian, House of White Birches nostalgia archives

At last it was 5 o'clock and time to dash into the living room to see what Santa had left them. Father was there already, and had the candles glowing brightly on the tree.

The little boys ran for their toys; there were only a few this year. After watching and laughing with them for a while, the girl went to look for her own gifts. She looked around but saw nothing except her Christmas stocking hanging over her chair. She glanced at her mother and saw her watching with sadness and anxiety in her eyes. The father was helping the little ones with their toys and pretended not to see the questioning look on his only daughter's face.

Forcing herself to smile, she dove into the contents of the stocking. There were some lovely candies and nuts, a large red apple and an orange, and in the very tip of the stocking, a small package. Smiling, she pulled it out and carefully tore the wrapping off. In the small box was a lovely bracelet with blue stones in a silver setting; it was inexpensive, but very, very lovely.

"Oh, how pretty! It will just match the dress you made me for my birthday, Mama!" she said.

Tears filled the mother's eyes and her anxiety seemed to fade a bit. The father also looked relieved. "It's not very much, Honey, but being out of work this year … ."

And then, all of a sudden, the awful truth hit the young girl: This *was* her Christmas this year! There were no other gifts! It was at that very moment that she began to realize what the word "Depression" really meant. She sadly reflected on how things had changed since her father had lost his job; how there were fewer luxury goodies around the house, fewer new clothes, more "making do." She knew that somehow she was being tested.

"It's the very nicest gift I could ever want. I love it!" Then she gave each parent a hug before turning her attention to her two younger brothers to hide her tears of disappointment.

It was the family tradition to always go to Grandpa and Grandma's home for Christmas dinner. All the aunts, uncles and cousins came bringing fun and their food specialties.

The mother had prepared her best dishes and soon had everything ready. The father loaded the sled with mysterious boxes and they set out for Grandma's house only a few blocks away.

They had gone only one short block, however, before they stopped. The mother said, "We'll be stopping a minute while your daddy takes this small box of goodies into Mr. Ross and Louie."

Mr. Ross and Louie were close neighbors. Mrs. Ross had died a long time ago and the girl knew there was no mother in the house for Louie.

"What's in the box?" the young girl asked.

"Well, just some bread, a little fruitcake and the chicken we fixed for them. There are some apples and a bit of candy. It's not much this year, but it will help brighten the day for them."

How can they be giving things away? the young girl thought. *They don't even have enough for themselves.* But she remembered other Christmas mornings when she had played with her toys while the father had gone around with boxes, visiting all the neighbors. Giving was vitally important to him.

Another three blocks down the road, they stopped again, this time to visit old Mr. Kreykendall. He was a strange man; even his name was strange. He lived all alone, and sometimes the kids were scared of him. But Father had said he was kind and wouldn't even hurt a flea; he was just a lonely old man. After the goody box was left, Mr. Kreykendall followed the father out to the gate, thanked the family and wished them a Merry Christmas. He invited them to come back sometime.

Just a couple of blocks from Grandma's house lived another strange person that all the kids called "crazy." She used to wear an old scarf around her thin hair, and she sometimes jumped out of the bushes and scared the kids as they walked home from school. But that didn't bother the mother and father. They stopped and left the last box with her. When they left, "Crazy Kate" was peering through her grimy window, smiling and waving at them.

At Grandma's house, all was laughter, talk and excitement as they put the dinner on the table. It was a very small, pioneer-type home, there since the early days of the little town. It had always been full of people, warmth and love. Grandma was always certain she had food enough for everyone and one or two besides. If anyone came while they were eating, she would say, "Pull up a chair and have a bite with us." And if the person hesitated, Grandfather would say, "Come on! There's aplenty! If there's room in the heart, there's room in the house! Pull up a chair!" And they usually did.

I know about all of this because, you see, I

At last it was 5 o'clock and time to dash into the living room to see what Santa had left them. Father was there already, and had the candles glowing brightly on the tree.

was that young girl, and that mother and father were my dear parents and those little boys were my two little brothers. Those were my neighbors who received the goody boxes and it was to my grandparents' home that we went on that long-ago Christmas.

I tell you this story because this was the Christmas I really grew up. I was 12 at the time. Afterward, as I lay in my bed reviewing the fun of the day, I remembered my early morning disappointment, but I still felt the love of my parents' hugs! I saw again the happiness on the faces of a lonely neighbor and his young son when someone remembered them on Christmas, the thanksgiving and joy in an old man's heart because he knew that he had a good friend, and the toothless grin of an old lady as she waved through a dirty windowpane to her friends.

I felt again the warmth and love that flowed all through Grandmother's kitchen as family gathered to share what they had. It was then that I realized Christmas was a joyous time of loving, caring and sharing. That night I made a promise to myself that I would like to make my family's Christmas just like it. I would make it a time to share what I had with someone who had need of a friend.

Many Christmas seasons have come and gone since then, but I am happy to say I have kept my promise. We've had many kinds of Christmases in the ensuing years: when there was sickness, when someone's chair was empty at the table, when we were richer, or much poorer. But there has never been a Christmas without goody boxes! The little silver and blue bracelet is long gone, but the great lesson of sharing and caring that it taught me has never been forgotten.

And it all began with one memorable Christmas in a valley town in the Wasatch Mountains. ❖

Making a Miracle

By Mrs. Joe R. Baker

The Great Depression of the late 1930s was still plaguing our country when my husband, Joe, accepted a pastoral call to the Baptist church in a small county seat in eastern Oklahoma.

I'll never forget my first view of the church building. It was nothing but a dull, gray, concrete basement with a bare skeleton of blackened framework above it—witches' fingers against a formidable sky.

Twice before, former pastors had attempted to lead the congregation in building a sanctuary above the basement, but each time the effort was thwarted by a lack of sufficient funds to continue the work. Over time the green-timbered framework warped and blackened through inclement weather and swayed in the winter winds, mocking the people as they came to worship in the forlorn basement.

As the Depression droned on, the church members became resigned to their failures and accepted the derisive title that had been given them by the community: "those underground Baptists."

This appellative cut to the bone each time my husband and I heard it. We tried to dismiss it from our minds and to think of constructive ways to present a pleasant and inviting image to the community.

With an eagerness and zeal he hoped would be contagious, Joe attacked the gigantic responsibility of restoring vision, bolstering faith and arousing enthusiasm for raising enough money to build an attractive place to worship.

For months the people reacted like a small child who has had his fingers burned by touching a hot stove. They were reluctant to even *visualize* a completed sanctuary. With a fatalistic attitude, everyone seemed to think, *What's the use?*

At home we prayed and planned and persevered. Then, in the fullness of time, God answered our prayers in a totally unexpected manner.

One day while I was attending a missionary meeting, Joe remained at home with our two small children, who were napping. As he sat studying there was a knock at the door. Joe invited in a stranger who identified himself as being from an adjoining county.

"What do you underground Baptists intend to do about that old building?" he blurted.

"Well," my husband said apologetically, "I haven't made much headway yet, but I keep remembering the words from Proverbs: 'Where there is no vision, the people perish.' And I'm hoping and praying they will soon be able to visualize by faith a new sanctuary and make new commitments to start—and to complete—the work. God will have to make a miracle in their hearts first."

"I'm glad to hear that," the stranger said. "In my work I pass here often, and every time I look at that spectral place, I moan with grief.

"This week I've received a thousand dollars extra money, and ordinarily I'd put my tithe of $100 in my own church Sunday morning, but on my way home I felt God leading me to give that tithe to your church. So here's a check to start your building program."

The check was received graciously and thankfully. On Sunday morning when Joe told the congregation of the stranger who cared enough to give, the Lord gave the vision needed in the hearts of the people.

As in Nehemiah's day, they had a mind to work. The task was not easy. Money was scarce, but it came in week by week, bit by bit, as faith increased, until the building was completed.

The stranger's gift was like a bit of yeast, leavening the whole lump. ❖

The Good Samaritan

By Sam Hieronymus II

*I*f my poor head were a jukebox, I'd be playing records indiscriminately, musically narrating the sordid story of the 1930s in all its incomparable severity. The oppressive heat and prolonged drought of 1983 brought it all back in lucid clarity. Procuring a dollar during the Great Depression of the early 1930s was as difficult as making the Olympic team. The profound desire of the poor to become rich knew no bounds. But poor folks back then did without what people on welfare today take for granted as their God-given, inalienable right. For some, their lifestyles were reduced to the equivalent of drinking muddy water and sleeping in a hollow log.

In the midst of these desperate circumstances, I actually came into possession of a great big $20 bill in the summer of 1930. It was the most exhilarating experience of my young life, and it provided me with a tiny taste of quality living. I went to a county square dance one night with that $20 bill burning a hole in my pocket. I became something of a celebrity as I drank my fill of soda pop, ate ice-cream cones like they were going out of style, and danced all night—and all for free, because the lady running the establishment didn't have enough money to make change!

I found out that good old Mr. Abell had given up his job with the pipeline company so I could work and make enough to buy groceries for my family.

But if it had not been for a fine old man named Mr. Abell, it might well have been years before my groping hands felt the luxury of a $20 bill.

Mr. Abell was poor, a farmer's hired man. When he worked, he worked like a dog for 12 hours a day. Then, when the corn was laid by and the hay was all put up, there was little for him to do, and he was temporarily unemployed. He never received but $1 a day for his prodigious efforts, but he and his wife made that meager wage stretch further than young folks would ever believe today.

But poor though he might be, Mr. Abell was something else: He was a humanitarian.

The Panhandle Eastern Pipeline Co. brought its first pipeline to our area in 1930 and went about the business of installing pipelines to the homes of Houstania, Mo. They were hiring laborers and there were plenty of willing applicants, for they were reported to pay big bucks. The company chose the most robust men available, men willing and able to swing a pick and shovel with gusto. A job with them could mean a dramatic change in my dreary lifestyle—if they would only give me one.

But, at 17 and suffering the ravages of malnutrition, I didn't look very muscular. The pipeline foreman cut me down to size when he told me I was too young and didn't have enough hair on my chest. His uncouth comment sparked raucous laughs from the waiting crowd, and I was mad enough to fight a buzz saw! But this didn't deter me from asking him for a job day after day. I told him that I could do a man's work, but he grew more obnoxious as the days passed. It took a lot of fortitude to face that foreman each day, but somehow I managed it. It took a lot out of me.

I lived with my mother and sister, and we existed on incredibly short rations. Mr. and Mrs. Abell were our neighbors, and they became aware of our unfortunate circumstances when they walked in unannounced one day at noon. They were shocked to see that we had practically nothing to eat. We wouldn't have had them know this for the world, and it bothered us immensely that they were aware of our sorry circumstances.

Mr. Abell was poor, a farmer's hired man. When he worked, he worked like a dog for 12 hours a day.

Meanwhile, I kept showing up at the pipeline company each day, asking that obnoxious foreman for work. And each day I was rebuffed. I held out some faint hope, though; Mr. Sneathen, an old sharecropper who had obtained a job with the company, promised me that he would see that I got his job if he conked out.

He perspired profusely as he wielded the pick and shovel. His face got red as a beet and I heard him groan sometimes. I stood around all day, waiting like a turkey buzzard for the old man to drop. He stuck it out, though, and when he stayed, my last hope petered out.

Everyday I returned home from job seeking to hopelessness and not much else. My mom and sister ran out to meet me expectantly, but I always had only bad news for them.

We didn't know what electricity was, but that wasn't a problem; we never gave *that* luxurious notion a thought. We carried water from a spring a quarter-mile from the house and accepted it as a normal living condition. We cooked and heated with firewood, and kerosene lamps were very much in vogue.

We were not the least distressed by this mode of existence. Our greatest problems were lack of adequate food and clothing. And another giant stalked us unmercifully, contributing to our anxiety. We didn't know from one year to the next whether we would have a place to live.

The only farms we could rent were so run-down that no one else would rent them. The shacks we were forced to live in were eyesores, though Mom always did her best to make them livable. She had a trite expression that we didn't like: "Beggars can't be choosers." She always said it with a wry smile, though, for she knew that we would *never* beg.

We were definitely in dire straits that sizzling summer of 1930. It looked as though any pretense of luck had finally ran out when some young chickens saved the day. Mom had raised chickens that spring. Normally we wouldn't have eaten them when they were still so small, but now they were all the food we had. There was no lard for frying them so she baked them in the oven of the old Home Comfort cookstove. That baked chicken was not very appetizing. I hated it, but it kept us from starving.

We were not plagued by being overweight, as so many are today. I kept a ball peen hammer and nail handy for those frequent occasions when I needed to make a new hole in my leather belt. I often wondered if people in hell had it any worse.

I had a king-size mountain of frustrated desires. I wanted to go places and do things! I wanted to live life to the full! I was willing and anxious to work for peanuts to realize a tidbit of my ambitions, but no one seemed to want me. They all thought I was too young, I suppose. I felt like an outcast and wondered to what useful purpose I had been born.

One morning I went through the motions of asking the taciturn foreman for a job, the same as I had every day, for so long. I had a terrific shock when the loud-mouthed man bellowed, "You're hired, Bub!" I couldn't believe my good fortune.

That job was long completed and I had long since spent all my earnings when I found out that good old Mr. Abell had given up *his* job with the pipeline company so I could work and make enough to buy groceries for my family.

Mr. Abell has gone to his reward now, but I'm sure he acquired immeasurable treasure in heaven for the wonderful deed he did for me, my mother and my sister. ❖

No Empty Seats

By Waldo V. Pettenati

"There's room for three," my mother's voice whispered into the bedroom.

Oh, no! Not today again, I thought. I knew "room for three" meant Emma Hendrickson had called across the yard to say that Bessie Scanlan telephoned at 7:30 a.m. Three of us had to be up and ready for church. Didn't Mrs. Scanlan ever tire of going to church? Why'd she always pick on us? Hoping to shut off the voice, I stuffed the pillow around my ears.

"Aw, Ma, not me," I begged, rolling over, half asleep.

"Call Yolanda. I'll go get Mrs. Graziano and Anna." At the same time, I fell into a comfortable world of unconsciousness.

When I awakened after what I thought was hours, I found the kitchen empty and quiet. My mother had found someone to fill the empty seats. I was pleased and yet I felt guilty, for I had disappointed her and Yolanda again. While I was sleeping soundly, they were either on the road or in church with the Scanlans. *I'm glad I'm not with them,* I thought, but I knew that I would hear, "It's your turn tomorrow, sleepy or not."

It was 1930, and I lived with my parents, five sisters and two brothers in northwestern Pennsylvania in an old, ramshackle house, weather-washed and sun-faded gray. Our timeworn home stood apologetically between Emma Hendrickson's and Anna Benson's respectable homes. Emma and Anna, local merchants, owned two of the seven telephones in Crosby, Pa.; we were within yelling distance of their front porches.

During the Depression, neighbors knew and cared for each other. This notion of caring was evidenced by taking someone along to fill empty seats. There was a concern for neighbors, but there was also a concern that empty seats were not wasted in an automobile to and from points of travel. The number of needed passengers was determined by the number of seats to be filled. Our family became regular passengers on those early morning trips in the Scanlans' McFarland limousine, the mechanical behemoth, which lumbered back and forth between Colegrove, Crosby and St. Elizabeth's in Smethport.

"Converts take their religion seriously," my sister Yolanda often reminded me. But Bessie Scanlan really took her conversion to Catholicism too seriously for us. We kids thought she ought to live in church. It would have saved a lot of traveling back and forth the 10 miles. My mother, of course, thought otherwise. For her, going to church was the only diversion from the chore of rearing eight children.

Mrs. Scanlan went to Mass daily and sometimes attended two masses on Sunday. She was sure to attend every Holy Day of Obligation and important feast days, retreats and All Souls' Day. Special novenas—for whatever—found Mrs. Scanlan in church. Consequently for us kids it meant that the Scanlan limousine, with its three rows of brown leather seats and two small ones that dropped from the sides had to be occupied.

The McFarland limousine was a rare species. It was a slightly modified version of a World War I tank, which consented to function only at the hands of Herman Lord, a stern, no-nonsense-from-you-kids driver who maneuvered the cumbersome machine over the unpaved road to Smethport. "It has 18 spark plugs," Mr. Lord would boast to anyone who would listen. "Three for each cylinder—two for ignition and one for exhaust."

The old car would skid to a stop a few feet past us on the gravel road. My eyes always caught the large, black letters on the radiator: "MCFARLAND SIX." I thought it was the most elegant automobile around, and I felt grand and royal in it. Its tufted leather seats projected a plushness that was otherwise absent in our lives.

Before the McFarland left the Scanlan garage in Colegrove for Smethport, it meant an early morning, 7:30 a.m. telephone call. We were expected to be lined up along the roadside when the sputtering limousine arrived. In rain, snow or heavy dew, we saw the old car, its winged-ball radiator cap moving toward us. No sooner had the McFarland crunched to a stop than two heavy doors opened and we heard, "Holy cow, Ma! Do we have to stop for everybody in town?"

"Now children," Mrs. Scanlan would respond softly, "we don't mind. There's always room for one more. It would be a shame to drive all the way to Smethport with empty seats." I wondered why empty seats were such a shame, but just as if nothing had been said, we were on our way to Smethport.

The ride to St. Elizabeth's Church was usually uneventful except for the conversation. The Scanlan children dared to say things we Pettenatis only thought about. The conversation intrigued me.

"We get hot chocolate today at Mrs. Garey's shop, don't we? Huh, Ma?" one of the Scanlans would begin.

"Yes, children. Did you get your nickel from the kitchen table?" Mrs. Scanlan's tone was quiet; a rosary bead fell from her thumb and index finger, her lips moved in a piano-hammer motion of Hail Marys, which was interrupted with, "After Mass, Mr. Lord will stop at the Garey Shop," and again her lips and fingers began the motion of prayer and bead.

Few cars were on the road 7:30 in the morning. I always sat upright and still in the old car, anticipating each passing landmark—past the Grazianos with everybody asleep, and on and on to the red brick church of St. Elizabeth.

Hushed into silence, we genuflected, blessed ourselves, said a prayer, blessed ourselves again, looked around and pushed slowly into Mrs. Scanlan's rented, highly varnished pew which, to her great satisfaction, was filled with Scanlans and Pettenatis.

Sounds and echoes in the church lulled me into a chin-dropping sleep. The white marble altar of niches, tall, gold candleholders, flower vases and covered chalice became my imaginary labyrinth. Small red and blue vigil lights at the station of St. Therese flickered between burning and going out. The swaying flames hypnotized me and the pleasant odor of incense made me comfortable.

Except for the hard edges of the wooden kneelers, I was content that I had come along. The warmth of the clanking steam radiators, the bright lights and the colorful vestments of Father Barrett made me secure with the Mass and the people around me.

The clunk of kneelers indicated latecomers. Coughs, throat clearing and nose honking bounced off the wainscoted walls and then rose, echoing to the high arched ceiling. Suddenly the jingling communion bell jarred me back into the real world. I remained there until Father Barrett turned slowly and gracefully and, with hands outstretched to bless, intoned, "*Ite missa est.* Go, the mass is finished."

After Mass we dashed across the street to Mrs. Garey's Shop. Mrs. Scanlan remained in church to complete the 14 Stations of the Cross, or to say special prayers before the flickering red and blue vigil lights. She would rejoin us with an inexpressible reflection of peace, which had contemplated the mystery of heaven, and which was soon to be dimmed by someone.

Once inside the Garey Shop, we pushed each other for a stool at the long, white marble counter. Meanwhile, Mrs. Garey had placed a cup

and saucer of hot chocolate before each of us and carefully dropped into the steaming brown liquid one marshmallow. Suddenly, from the far end of the counter came, "Mrs. Garey, you know, if we went to McCoy's Drugstore we'd get real whipped cream in our hot chocolate."

Mrs. Garey stood still, smoothed her apron with both hands and faced her tormentor. "You can have a saltine cracker with the cocoa, if you like, children." She returned to place one cracker on each saucer.

Young Nicholas Scanlan contributed to most of the venturesome conversation. Teen-aged Nicholas was a tormentor, not only of those whom he met in church, but of his mother in particular. Often he boxed her into a corner of exasperation with his playful remarks.

Sometimes, if there was nothing else to dwell on, Nicholas would enliven the conversation by venturing into the world of Latin Mass.

In the 1930s, the altar boys and the choir responded to Father Barrett reciting the Mass. The faithful in their pews were busy with rosaries; some thumbed through missals, others recited prayers which granted plenary indulgences for the poor souls in purgatory. Nicholas would begin, "Ma, you know when the choir up in the loft answers Father Barrett with '*Agnus Dei,*' what they're saying is 'onions daily.'" And we smirked to think that he had thought of such a close rhyme.

Mrs. Scanlan's corrective retort was the closest she ever came to being impatient with her son. "Why Nicholas William Scanlan! You know that is sacrilegious."

"And, Ma, you know when Father Barrett calls out, '*Dominus Vobiscum,*' he's really saying 'Dominic wants a biscuit,'" and we covered our mouths not to explode in laughter at Nicholas' interpretation of words we considered sacred.

Dashing back to the McFarland, we sat in the same seats that we had occupied on the way to church. Even before Mr. Lord ground on the starter, the sparring dialogue began.

"Mother, Father Barrett did not say that tomorrow was the Feast of St. Therese," one of the Scanlan girls proclaimed.

"Now children, wait until tomorrow morning and we'll see what develops," Mrs. Scanlan said in her soft, prayer-tone voice, and a bead dropped to complete a decade in the loop forming on her lap.

"Yeah, we know what will develop tomorrow. Why can't we sleep in like the other kids?" came from two parts of the car simultaneously.

I was not bothered by the chatter. I was caught up in the ride home. The disturbing thought of being awakened in the morning was far, far away.

"Now, children," Mrs. Scanlan would respond, "this is no way to act in front of Mrs. Pettenati. You know we will decide in the morning," and she winked at my mother. Yes, we knew what she would decide in the morning. Another 7:30 call, another trip to St. Elizabeth's with no empty seats—but who cared? I thought to myself, *I'll find someone to fill in for me.* It was a chance worth taking.

As we continued homeward, I tried to forget the Mass, the Scanlans and filling empty car seats. I hoped that my brother Herbert had milked the cows. If he had not, I would have to and I was hungry because I had fasted for communion. I wanted to eat, to play ball, and go to the woods. I didn't want to know about a tomorrow that might bring another saint's day. Still, as we lumbered along, a disturbing inner voice kept infesting my mind. Half awake, I heard my mother's call, "There's room for five. Mrs. Scanlan telephoned." And a silent voice responded, "Oh, no, not *five!* I'll get Mrs. Grazzie and Anna, Olga Marinik and Josephine, and Ma. That's five. It's what? The Feast of St. Therese?" My 10-year-old mind was devastated with thoughts, which kept interfering with play.

Rain splatters against the windshield and the *swish-swash* of the wipers' arcs exposed the brilliant foliage of the Pennsylvania hillsides. Fifty years have passed since the 7:30 morning calls across the yard. I seldom drive by Bessie Scanlan's home without sensing fragments of nostalgia, which at age 10, I was sure were immutable. These nostalgic reprints of the 1930s were natural routines that I could count on to last forever, but which changed into a life that I came to accept. Life appeared static, at times confusing, sometimes dull, and often times, surprising. Outwardly, Bessie Scanlan accepted life with little trepidation. She and my mother influenced me to accept the ambiguities I was to encounter.

There are no McFarlands on the road from Colegrove to Crosby to Smethport today; most of the cars zipping along the old highway have empty seats. "Onions daily" and "Dominic wants a biscuit" have faded into a past, forgotten generation, faded with the nostalgic fragments that I had counted on to last forever. The hot chocolate, the marshmallow and the one saltine cracker have given way to a slice of hot, cheese-dripping pizza and a glass of iced Coke.

The wind scatters maple leaves across the graves of Bessie Scanlan and Nicholas on St. Elizabeth's Cemetery. Their graves are not far from my mother and father's, where the chiseled tombstones cast light shadows at midday. Whenever I traverse the plots of St. Elizabeth's, my mind never ceases to recast the gravestone markers.

And then, be it a breeze or a passing intuitive thought, I hear, "Now children, you know it would be a shame to drive all the way to Smethport with those seats empty."

And I hear the response, "Oh, no, not *five!* I'll go get … ." ❖

Always Room

By Margaret V. Davis

During the Great Depression we lived on a 360-acre farm. There were 10 in our family—seven girls and a boy, plus Mom and Dad. We lived in a four-bedroom home with a front room and kitchen. My dad's philosophy was, "There is always room for one more." Dad always made room for travelers who stopped while making their way across the country.

We took Arch and Lily into our home; they stayed for six months. While Arch and Lily lived with us, Lily made a German dish for supper that was a noodle-like mixture crumbled in hot milk. When spring came, they left and we never heard from them again.

Once, when it was snowing, a man came to the door late in the evening. Dad and Mom had gone to town in the lumber wagon. But, with Dad's philosophy in mind, we kids took him in.

When Dad came into the house, there sat the man, getting warm beside the heating stove. To Dad's surprise, when he opened the *Oklahoma Farmer Stockman,* he saw the man's picture. The man was wanted by the law for breaking out of prison.

Dad stayed up all night with a shotgun by his side in case he came out of the bedroom. We children had no idea what was going on. Later, after the stranger left, we learned why Dad was very cautious of the man's actions.

When the stranger went to the supper table, he carried his coat with him. The next morning the stranger just dressed, went out the door and headed south, the same way he had come.

Mom went out and called to him that he was leaving in the same direction from which he had come. She had him come back and have breakfast before he went on his way, which he did. That was the last we ever heard of him.

Next came Robert Jennings, his wife and baby, who stayed for a while. I cannot remember how long they stayed, but after they left we never heard from them again.

With eight children and Mom and Dad, we children had to share our already overcrowded beds so the strangers could have a room to themselves. Can you imagine the joy of three sleeping in one bed—two at the head and one trying to sleep across the foot? We were feeling hard times, but we didn't know it. ❖

Grandmother's Boardinghouse

By G. Arney Prayter

I can't help thinking that there must be thousands of people who have never *heard* of a boardinghouse, let alone seen one. But I was reared in a boardinghouse in Toledo, Ohio. My mother had died when I was 4 years old, and my maternal grandmother lived across the street from us. She earned a living by opening her home to boarders. We did have an occasional roomer, but that was rare. Most of Grandma's boarders were gentlemen, away from home and working in Toledo, or perhaps looking for work. My grandmother had a reputation for being a fine cook, and the boardinghouse was always full.

During the Depression, however, when things were really critical, some of the people couldn't pay when their rent was due. She never had the heart to "put them out." To the best of my knowledge, they paid her when they were able.

My father was a tool-and-die maker and sometimes he was the only wage earner in the house. There were times when, even with his skill, he couldn't find a job—or if he had been working, the company was unable to pay when payday rolled around. He would get paid eventually, but he couldn't depend on it when he really needed it.

During one of the bad times when Grandma didn't know quite how she was going to find enough food to put on the table, I found a dollar on the sidewalk. I hurriedly ran home with it and Grandma was thrilled. She said, "Oh, Sally! Now we can have potatoes for supper!"

Such was life in a boardinghouse in the Good Old Days.

I will never forget our dining room. Ten or 12 people had no trouble being seated comfortably around the table. My grandmother was very strict regarding meals. Meals were served three times daily. We never heard of "snacks." Woe be unto a child that might think he or she could check out the icebox. The iceman came by only a couple of times a week, and sometimes we didn't have the 10 cents or 25 cents for a block of ice. If we could only get a 25-pound block for 10 cents, it didn't last long, so it was quite important to keep the icebox door closed. For these obvious reasons, the cook was the only one allowed to open it.

Some of the boarders were like family to me. If there was any child abuse in those days, I never heard of it! Although children were to be "seen and not heard," they also were respected and cherished in a way that hardly exists anywhere today, regardless of economic status.

I remember a dear soul named Jack Ward who was like a grandfather to me. (My own were deceased.) He would rock me if I had measles, earache or whatever. Another of our boarders was from Ireland. He had a beautiful tenor voice. His name was Tommy Driscoll. He'd come home, pick me up in his arms and we'd wind up the old Victrola. Then he would sing *On the Road to Mandalay.* The world had so much more "true love" in it then, it seems to me.

We had many good times in those days. Even though most people hardly had two nickels to rub together, there was a kinship, a caring that I haven't experienced or seen since those old Depression days. I feel I learned tolerance, consideration and compassion for others—not to mention many skills necessary to be a homemaker—back in that boardinghouse.

Finally the boardinghouse closed and Grandmother spent her last days with my father, my brother and me—"the Three Musketeers," as we called ourselves.

I often think that it is a shame that in our present society we can no longer have boardinghouses where love abounds. ❖

© *Dominoes* by Jim Daly

We Didn't Know We Were Poor

Chapter 4

Some might think I am being more than a bit disingenuous when I say that most of us who survived and thrived back in the Good Old Days simply didn't know we were poor.

It wasn't that we were totally ignorant of our surroundings, but that we simply didn't think of ourselves as deprived. We were neither better off—nor for that matter worse off—than most of those family, friends and neighbors with whom we interacted. We ate about the same things, lived in about the same type of homes, went to the same small schools.

How did parents keep their children from the anguish of poverty? How did they insulate us, somehow granting us the gift of youthful bliss? I can't speak for all families, but in ours the answer came around the kitchen table and in the form of hours upon hours of playing dominoes.

How did dominoes play such a dominant role in our lives? It was a diversion from drab days that might otherwise have drowned hope. Looking back, I realize that Mama and Daddy used those evenings, oftentimes after a rather meager meal, to focus our thoughts on what we had, not what we didn't have.

Daddy had a job at the lumber mill, and brought home a paycheck, albeit small, to augment the living we were attempting to scratch out on that rocky Ozark Mountain hillside. Though he came home tired, especially after we finished evening chores, it seemed there was always time to clear the supper dishes and share a game of dominoes. There in the kitchen of the three-room shack we called home, the five of us set aside reality for a couple of hours, laughing our way through the day's events, finding a silver lining even on the darkest of life's clouds.

Oh, yes, there were other lessons learned at the domino table. While I never understood quantum physics (it wasn't taught at our small rural school), I developed a keen sense of mathematics and still can add large columns in my head, a skill that had its infancy in our games of dominoes. I learned to play by the rules of life, as well as the rules of dominoes, which in turn taught me the ways of peaceful coexistence, whether playing with family at the table or friends on the front porch.

But the greatest gift Mama and Daddy gave us with that cheap double-nine set of "bones" came in words unspoken and deeds unseen. They proclaimed, "Better days are coming. … Have faith. … Trust us, everything will work out fine."

Being poor was a state of mind in the Good Old Days. We didn't have a lot, but we had each other. And dominoes. It's no wonder we didn't know we were poor.

—Ken Tate

© *Snow Party* by John Sloane

I Didn't Know What Poor Meant

By Lucille Armstrong Anton

A farm was a terrific place for a kid to grow up, especially during the bleak days of the Depression.

Mom and Dad had plenty of worries, though—how to make the mortgage payments, whether the livestock lived or died, whether the farm machinery would run or not, and whether or not the weather would cooperate for harvesting the crops.

I turned 7 in 1929, the year of the crash, but I wasn't knowledgeable enough then to be aware of the hard times that followed for the next 10 years. My tummy was satisfied. Mom always had a big garden and cooked tremendously good meals. We lived on homemade bread and lots of her home-canned vegetables and fruits from the cellar. She had the energy to do that besides helping Dad with the haying.

Spending money was another thing. We had none. In order to get a few groceries now and then, we'd take eggs to the store and trade them for sugar, salt and flour, and receive a little cash to boot. I guess that is how the question originated, "Where do you trade?" Today, of course, that's an obsolete term.

At age 7, however, I thought I had everything. I had a swing. Oh, it was a dandy—a board seat with a hole in each end through which the rope passed. I spent hour upon hour swinging happily in the shade of the box elder tree. I also had a horse … well, I liked to *think* of her as being mine. She was an old nag to be sure, and near the end of her earthly journey. This mare had been my grandfather's and then my dad's. She was gentle with little kids and didn't seem to mind if two or three of us rode at a time.

Dad had better horses for the farm work as well as a handsome sorrel gelding that was his pride and joy. This beautiful animal trotted between the shafts of the cutter on many blustery, cold days. The little two-room schoolhouse was at a crossroads in the country a mile and a half away. School must go on, come cold or sleet or blizzard, so Dad tucked a heavy horse blanket around me and took me to school in the cutter. I liked to peek out once in awhile to see where we were. Sometimes the horseshoes sent small pieces of ice or snow stinging against my face, so I'd quickly cover up again and listen to the squeak of the runners on the snowy road.

Dad and Mom talked about the Depression, but I just accepted it as the way life was, I guess. As a result, I've grown to appreciate the little things and to be truly thankful for what we have.

Our Christmas stockings didn't get filled; nevertheless, I was excited to find an orange and a walnut in mine one Christmas morning. Then Mom asked, "Did you reach way in?" Glory be, there was a quarter, way down in the toe! Right about then my heart overflowed with happiness.

Winters brought special fun. Our "back 40" was hilly, a super place for sliding. I know it must have been a great sacrifice for my folks to buy that sled one winter, but I used it so much over the years that they surely knew how I valued it. I seemed to enjoy pulling it to the top as much as I liked the swift, breathtaking trips to the bottom again.

Other kids liked our hills, too. When we wanted to rest a bit, we'd lie on our backs on the snowy hillside and make "snow angels" in the snow, moving our arms back and forth to make the shapes of angel wings.

Skiing was a wonderful adventure too, once my feet grew big enough to stay in the straps on an old pair of homemade skis that had been standing in a corner in the woodshed for a few years. They were heavy and really too big for me, but that didn't keep me from practicing with them. When my Uncle Bill bought a pair of 5-footers, I was ecstatic.

Uncle Bill made his home with us. I guess he didn't pay anything for board and room, so maybe he felt that by giving my brothers and me something now and then, it would help my folks. We knew later that Dad couldn't afford luxuries such as skis.

Very often Uncle Bill had a candy bar tucked deep in his mackinaw pocket. I'd run to meet him when I saw him walking back from town and he'd say, "Put your hand in my pocket to keep warm," and that's what was there.

Uncle Bill and Dad took me along whenever they went hunting squirrels. I can see them yet, tiptoeing around a big oak, motioning for me to stay a little way behind them and to be quiet. The cornfield adjacent to the woods provided food for the squirrels, so the well-fed little critters were as tasty as chicken. And Mom knew how to fry them just right. Well, it got so I could aim the .22 rifle at the squirrels once in awhile and shoot; I got good enough that they even let me take the gun alone when I got older.

These walks in the woods fascinated me. No matter what month it was, I took never-ending delight in discovering interesting and exciting things. I knew where and when to look for the first mayflowers; violets grew around old rotting logs and brush piles—tall, stately, yellow ones and little, short, purple ones. Jack-in-the-pulpit was not an endangered species back then. Wild geraniums, trilliums (they are protected now) and bloodroots with their pure white blossoms all grew profusely in the rich, black soil. Most exciting of all was finding columbines.

I'll never forget the sweet tartness of the wild strawberries, and each year I remembered exactly where the patch was located. They were small, though, and it took so many to make a showing in the bucket. But Mom seemed glad to get them and we'd have a strawberry shortcake.

The wild raspberries ripened a little later. It was fun to pick those, though some years they had a tendency to be wormy, which detracted from my enthusiasm.

Finding blackberries was a completely different situation. Huge, luscious berries hung so thick that I'd dream about picking them all night long. The canes were long, almost like vines hanging to the ground. The briars snagged my clothes so I learned to wear my oldest blouses and slacks. But those berries were delicious, absolutely scrumptious, and they were so big that it didn't take long to get enough for a batch of jam.

We found gooseberries, too, but we didn't bother about them except to taste a few that were ready to eat and to experience the peculiar way they are made, with little prickly things on them. They were rather interesting but there were not enough of them to merit our taking any home.

When I went to pick the chokecherries, pin cherries and wild plums that grew by the line fence, Dad let me take Grandpa's faithful old mare hitched to the buggy. While she stood under the tree, eating grass, I could reach the cherries from the buggy and soon have a bucketful. This worked fine except for the time a rabbit came bounding out of the tall weeds and frightened the horse. I spilled a few of the cherries as we took off with a leap, but was fortunate not to get thrown out of the buggy.

Yes, I will always enjoy fond memories of the years I spent growing up on the farm. Some may have considered us poor, but we didn't know what poor meant. ❖

Memories in Ragtime

By Cleo Silvers

My grandmother had the most exceptional talent for making work appear to be fun and games. Grandma didn't con you into a job by threats or promises. She was a woman of few words. She conveyed the idea with a twinkle in her eyes, a secretive grin, or a few well-chosen remarks. What were a few scratches on your arms when you could already taste the delicious gooseberry pies and jam that would result from foraging for the fruit in those thorny bushes in the woods? So what if your back was tired and your fingers cold? Much nearer reality was that hickory-nut cake and mouth-watering fudge that would be the finale of your fall nutting expedition.

Those forays into the country to pick wild grapes were well worth the effort; generous doses of their delicious juice, squeezed and bottled as only Grandma could make it, would speed you on your way toward convalescence if you contracted a bad cold or bout of flu.

Touring the countryside with Grandpa at the wheel of the big old car with jump seats, my sisters and I never felt we were doing anything but having fun. If a trip was for any distance and lunchtime neared, Grandma had us on the lookout for a country school where we could eat the homemade bread-and-butter sandwiches, cold fried chicken and crisp sugar cookies she'd packed, all washed down with lemonade with slices of real lemon. When we asked why stop at a school, she said, "There's shade to eat in, a well for fresh water, a yard to run in, and two three-holers out back. What more could you want?"

Each time we moved to another house, the big boxes of rag balls went along to be stored in the attic. There we sometimes found them to be effective ammunition.

Sibling rivalry among seven girls often resulted in some slight exaggeration of our accomplishments. As we related our achievements to Grandma, she would listen carefully and then say, "Tsk-tsk, big I, little you."

When asked what she meant, she explained that "i" should always be little and "YOU" should be big. I didn't understand, but after awhile I realized she always said it when we were doing a little bragging and got carried away with our own importance. Then Grandma would cluck and say, "My, my, BIG I, little you."

Grandma was not given to clichés, but she did impress upon us the importance of "waste not, want not," and she assuredly believed that "idle hands are the devil's workshop." It was probably with this in mind that she launched us on a project that cheated the devil out of a lot of eager little helpers for many an hour. What germ of an idea gave birth to the plan I don't recall, but Grandma promised that she would pay to have a room-size rug woven for us if we would sew together the necessary rag strips that we wound into balls. A rug factory would transform the rags into a lovely, colorful rug.

We got the monumental task under way during school vacation. Equipped with threaded needles and brand-new thimbles, we sat on the floor in a circle at my mother's feet while she tore strips from a discarded garment. We were each given two, which we carefully overlapped about an inch and firmly stitched together. My mother tore garment after garment into strips as we industriously sewed them together, chattering about how grand the rug was going to be and where it would look best.

We were disappointed that the balls didn't multiply faster, but we kept at it. Every time Grandma came to visit, she would inspect our collection, assuring us that it would be no time at all before we had enough. Often during our sewing stints, we would gaze longingly at the empty lot next door and wish we could be off playing. Many times sewing carpet rags for an hour was the punishment doled out for some minor infraction of house rules.

With seven girls of varying ages, it could be expected that differences of opinion often arose. These altercations were dissolved quickly when a third party whispered, "You'd better quit fighting or we'll all have to sew carpet rags." My mother didn't waste any time finding out who started things.

We must have been the orneriest kids in Iowa, for the box of balls grew and grew until it was finally filled and another was started … and then another … and another. Grandma was impressed but never satisfied. We tried to talk her into sending what we had to get the factory started, but she wouldn't agree to it.

Each time we moved to another house, the big boxes of rag balls went along to be stored in the attic. There we sometimes found them to be effective ammunition, but after a few fast tosses across the attic, they would start to unroll. Then, loathe to see our efforts destroyed, we would quickly rewind them.

Friends and relatives contributed their old

cast-offs to our efforts. My mother was way ahead of us with a large box of torn strips ready for any emergency. We usually sat in a circle on the floor, and while we sewed, we passed the time by talking. Our favorite topic was, "What I'm going to do when I get big." Many times we told stories, and a good one was continued into a serial.

Eventually the carpet rag project petered out. I'm sure they made many a cozy nest for generations of mice. The thread rotted away and the rags were too thin and worn to ever have made a decent rug—which I now suspect my grandmother knew from the beginning.

> *My mother tore garment after garment into strips as we industriously sewed them together, chattering about how grand the rug was going to be and where it would look best.*

For a long time I felt that for once we had been conned by Grandma. All that work we had been tricked into and nothing to show for it! But as the years passed and I had some small girls of my own and often listened to their bored complaints of "What can we do? There isn't anything to do," I began to grin in retrospect as I thought of those long hours spent sewing carpet rags.

The time had not been wasted. We learned to sew, and we learned the value of getting along together. We developed the patience and ingenuity to find something to do whenever we had any free time. I'm sure there are other ways to teach these traits, but I can vouch for the fact that it was quick, effective and saved a lot of wear and tear on Mother.

If those rag balls had been woven into a rug, it would have been worn out and discarded long ago. And yet, as I see them, they are woven in fantasy into a magic carpet that can never fade or wear. Memories are the warp, and lessons in discipline and patience are the woof.

I have only to close my eyes and I'm back in that circle. I see "little 'I'" working on a magic carpet that "big 'YOU'"—my grandmother—instigated as a profitable way to keep 14 little hands from aiding and abetting the devil in his workshop. ❖

Rag Balls by Doug Knutson, courtesy of Apple Creek Publishing

Untaxed Inheritance

By Vivian M. Loken

Our family with five children enjoyed few luxuries when we lived in the country during the Great Depression of the 1930s. The grocery box fresh from town disappointed young inquisitors with its box of laundry soap, toilet soap, lard and matches. But—oh blessed truth!—we had no standards of comparison to make us feel poorer. Almost everyone we knew was in similar straits.

Once a kid came to school boasting that he had sponge cake every day and angel food cake on Sunday. We saw right through that; nobody confronted the miserable, pretentious liar, but we made furtive estimates about the family's chicken population and guessed the rest.

To give you an idea of our circumstances, a new curtain in the dining room was a real big occasion. Even the new gable on an ancient log granary made us strut with prosperity. One of the commending factors of our particular situation was that passersby couldn't see our clothesline from the main road. The patches on our pants and darning on long johns were thus private matters.

I didn't realize then, however, what a treasure of cleanliness we had.

There were 22 steps between the main floor of our house to the unheated bedrooms upstairs. The stairs were plain wood, probably pine, and the steady tread of footsteps wore a sag in the middle. Those steps were clean, however. I know because I took my turns scrubbing them.

And let me tell you about the dadoes on the lower kitchen walls and about the Swedish claw-leg kitchen table. The enameled wood dadoes sported a sharp cleft just below the topmost molding that was supposed to be ornamental, but about which I was strongly suspicious. In order to clean it, you had to run a table knife capped with cloth through the cleft. The only chance you had of coming up with enough gunk to prove your effort was if the person who did it last had done a poor job.

I remember being especially rebellious about cleaning the grooves in the claw-legged table. *Who in the world,* I stormed to myself, *is going to look at table legs?*

One of the biggest cleaning occasions of the year came just before threshing time, when the crew of neighboring men who helped came to dine as well as work. We did extra cleaning for days, giving the organ keys a second lick, buffing away all the grime around the doorknobs and polishing the nickel trim on the cookstove. All this for 15–20 men who came in to eat wearing bits of straw in their perspiration-soaked hair and whose eyes were circled with grime that persisted even after splashing at the wash bowl outside.

We knew, though, in the canny way of children, that whatever their appearance or preoccupation with the steaming food, the men were under expectation from their wives to report when they got home. For the most part, the same sharp eyes that spotted something amiss with Bell Cow's youngest heifer would have noted a lonely fluff of dust wandering near the floor molding of the dining room, or a cobweb twisting wistfully from a distant corner of the ceiling. The intent was not malicious. Rather, with few other diversions, discussion of the ways of neighbors was a constant.

A lot of years have passed. At last I see my inheritance. What my parents could not give me in property and wealth, they gave me in other riches. Cleanliness is, surely, a partner to godliness. Clean claw-legged tables, troughed-out dado grooves and scrubbed wooden stair steps shout to me across the decades. ❖

> *I remember being especially rebellious about cleaning the grooves in the claw-legged table.* **Who in the world, I stormed to myself, is going to look at table legs?**

Mama's Kindness

By Ross Princiotto

Growing up in the Depression years of the late 1920s and early 1930s was not easy, especially for large families. No food was plentiful, and meat was especially scarce. We never lacked for food in our home, but meat was not a staple; we couldn't afford it.

Mama, a tiny, feisty Sicilian, reared six of us all by herself. She rented rooms to boarders, most of them Spanish immigrants hoping to find work in America. But employment was down, and although the boarders did enjoy a better life, times were still tough for them, especially since they also had to learn a new language. Often Mama would forgo their rent until they could afford to pay, or she would accept partial payment until they found work. She frequently invited the boarders to eat supper with us, and we always shared gladly.

We were not destitute. We really did not know what being poor meant. In spite of the many restrictions and needs, we were a happy, contented family.

Mama was generous to all, but her children came first. Sometimes she would surprise us with gifts or sweets she had purchased with rent money that she had wisely set aside and hid from us. We loved her all the more for it.

I was 10. Being the youngest had its advantages: I was obviously spoiled and given more attention than my three brothers and two sisters. And, too, I was certain to get all the hand-me-downs from my older brothers—knickers, shoes, shirts, sweaters. I proudly wore big brother's shoes and pants.

As was her habit, Mama would prepare a hot lunch for me when I returned from school.

Being the youngest had its advantages: I was obviously spoiled and given more attention than my three brothers and two sisters.

Cold snacks packed in a tin lunch box was not her idea of a healthy lunch for her little boy. One particular Monday, even as she washed her family's laundry and that of the boarders, she surprised me by making a special lunch for me, one that I'm sure she planned for days.

When I got home from school, there on the kitchen table sat a dish of mashed potatoes made with fresh milk and real butter, a thick slice of Italian bread, some strawberry jam (my favorite) and a tall glass of milk.

As I sat down to eat, Mama smiled. *What had she been up to on this very busy Monday morning wash day that occasioned a smile?* I wondered.

I began eating my mashed potatoes, took a large bite of bread and jam and sipped some milk. Then it happened!

I cut into the big serving of mashed potatoes with my fork and there, hidden under the potatoes, was a large wiener. What a treat!

How pleased Mama was when I made the discovery. "*Bon appetite*," she said as I cleaned my plate, saving the treat until last.

"*Ti amo*," I replied, giving Mama a kiss and a big hug.

I still remember Mama's smile that day when I discovered the wiener hidden under the heap of potatoes. You know, when I think about it, the Depression days weren't all that hard, thanks to Mama. ❖

Growing Up in the Depression

By Myrtle Jones

s young children growing up on a farm, my two sisters and I didn't realize that we were poor. When children have loving parents and plenty to eat and a place to sleep at night, they have no problem.

We lived in a big old white house on a hill overlooking my father's land and a large pecan orchard. Sometimes that pecan orchard kept us in necessities when other crops failed.

It didn't bother us that we had no modern facilities. We never had had any, and you don't miss something you've never had.

Our water came from a well just a short distance from the back porch. We had an outhouse, but it wasn't fancy—no colorful paint on the outside and no pictures inside. It did have the two customary holes, but both were the same size—not a big one for adults and a little one for children. Mostly I remember how cold it was trying to get to the outhouse with a foot of snow on the ground.

Everyone lived the same way we did, or so I thought. I discovered later just how wrong I was.

There was always plenty of food as far as I can remember, because my folks raised everything from vegetables and fruit of all kinds to chickens, cows and pigs. Mother canned about everything that was perishable; without electricity, there were no freezers or refrigerators.

Around Thanksgiving each year, Dad would butcher two or three big, fat hogs. The weather had to be cold enough so the meat would cure, not spoil. Dad invited two or three neighbors and their wives for what we called hog-killing day. The men would kill and dress out the hogs, then cut the meat into hams, shoulders, ribs and different cuts of meat. The meat was then placed on a large table in the smokehouse and covered with a sugar cure mixture.

While the men were taking care of the meat, the women were preparing a real feast that included fresh meat and my mother's chocolate pies. This is the way we almost always celebrated Thanksgiving. Each neighbor would take home several pounds of fresh meat in pay for their help.

Our lives went along as smooth as silk until I became a teenager in high school. We rode the bus to a consolidated school in a small town. These high schools were called "consolidated" because all the small country schools had been consolidated—or joined—with the high school.

My best friend lived north of school and I lived east. She was forever insisting that we spend the night with each other. Finally my mother consented for me to go home with her. I packed a small paper bag (overnight bags were unheard of) and boarded her bus for an overnight visit. The weather was hot, the bus was crowded and the distance was unending, as she lived miles out in the country.

Finally the bus pulled to a stop beside a barbed-wire fence. All one could see for miles was a pasture with a few scrubby cattle and a small house about a quarter-mile away in the pasture. I thought, *Surely she doesn't live way down there in that little house!* But when I saw her stand to exit, I knew that was it.

We were met at the yard by two or three small children and several barking dogs. Chickens were pecking around in the yard, unconcerned by our arrival.

We entered the living room, or "front room," as most people called them in those days. I was stunned to say the least; all this room contained was a bed, a dresser, a stand table and a few cane-bottom chairs. The stand table held the coal-oil lamp and a Bible.

My friend's bedroom was even more sparsely furnished, with only a bed, a chair and a string across one corner for hanging her clothes. The mattress on her bed was stuffed with corn shucks.

My friend's bedroom was even more sparsely furnished, with only a bed, a chair and a string across one corner for hanging her clothes. The mattress on her bed was stuffed with corn shucks. Lots of people used straw to fill the ticking for a bottom mattress, but they used a cotton mattress on top of the straw one. All these people had were shuck beds and they were hard as a rock.

Their kitchen was equally bare, containing only a wood-burning cookstove and a table with a long bench on each side and a cane-bottom chair at each end. The cabinets were boxes nailed to the wall.

In spite of these eye-openers, I enjoyed my visit. And I went home a more grateful daughter than I had been the day before. I realized that a lot of people had less than we did. Before I never thought of our family as poor; now I knew just how well-off we were. ❖

Apple Days

By Elsie Hamilton Mallory

For a couple of weeks I had been ready. The air had taken on that crisp autumn flavor, brisk enough to excite us kids but not cold enough to keep us inside.

Now I stood on our back steps, watching the western sky. Thin red and purple bars stretched across the sky as the sun crept downward as slowly as it possibly could. Tomorrow we were going to the apple orchard, and I couldn't wait!

The Depression was on and we were a large family—Dad, Mom, two boys and four girls. My younger brother Garnett and I were more trouble than all the other kids put together!

But "apple days" were a time to be excited anyway. For a few weeks we could enjoy some delicious treats that came along only once a year—pecans, peanuts, popcorn and apples. All year long we made do with what we had; supper was often just gravy and bread. So it was time we had some snacks!

We got our treats on Saturday nights, after our baths. We wrapped up and sat around the stove, munching hot popcorn and crisp, cold apples. The next night, Sunday, was homework night; Dad sharpened all our pencils with his pocketknife, and we would sit in a group surrounded by open books and paper. So Saturday night was our one night of freedom. However, we earned the snacks we got.

Picking up pecans in the nearby town of Brunswick was the least fun of our autumn adventures. It was tedious. We spent the afternoon bent over, picking up ripened pecans that had fallen from the trees. We couldn't eat any because we couldn't crack them. We did try, even though Mom warned us, "You'll break your teeth!" So we worked, Dad paid the man who owned the grove, and we went home, exhausted.

We raised peanuts in our garden. We really didn't want to eat these as we picked them, since they were the roots of the plant and dirt-covered when first pulled up. But once I simply got too eager. I cracked open the shell and popped the peanuts into my mouth, only to discover that they were raw—and mealy tasting. From then on, I waited until Mom had toasted them in the oven.

Finally our day arrived to go to the apple orchard. It was a long way, clear to Dalton, Mo., but it was a fun trip. And it was an all-day affair, so we packed a picnic lunch before we piled into the car. It was like a little vacation.

The work, at least for us kids, was minimal and delightful. We picked up some good apples off the ground, but most of them were picked right off the trees. We kids would sink our teeth into the juicy apples whenever we wanted and munch away. It was like getting all the free candy we wanted.

Many families that had come to pick apples brought trucks. We had to do the best with we could with our car. Dad poured the apples onto the floorboard of the car. We even had to sit on them on the way home! Fortunately, they were firm and didn't squish.

The real work with the apples was waiting for Mom the next day. Then our house looked like an apple-processing factory. If the weather was warm, Dad would build a big Indian fire and hang our big iron pot over the fire from a set of teepee poles. That's where the apple butter was cooked. We kids clamored around the hot iron pot, screeching and whooping like we were wild Indian warriors. Poor Mom was slaving over the hot mixture, trying to stir the thick stuff.

We also dried apples. Dad built five shallow trays with screens for the bottoms. If it was warm, these could be filled with sliced apples and placed in the sun. If weather didn't permit, the trays fit perfectly in the oven. On those days, Mom cooked the apple butter in big pots on top of the stove, and the kitchen got as hot and steamy as a factory.

We put some whole apples in the cellar to keep them during the winter. They stayed cold and crisp down there.

Apple days marked the beginning of winter, but it was a good time for us. Even though it was during the Depression, we six children had snacks for weeks. For us, depression didn't exist! ❖

Christmas Calamity

By Eric McDonald
as told to J.B. Cearley

The weather had remained nice all fall on the high plains of West Texas until the week before Christmas. In spite of the terrible Dust Bowl, we had made a crop. It was skimpy, but making any kind of crop in 1933 was unexpected because it forgot to rain in most of the nation for several years.

Our farm was on Highway 87, a few miles from Tulia. We worked the farmland with four mules and three sharp hoes. In the fall we gathered scraggly cotton and headed the maize by hand, tossing it into a wagon to haul to the barns.

When we had gathered our crops, my older sister, brother and I started back to school. Studying our books was a welcome vacation from dragging a heavy cotton sack along half-mile rows. School was exciting for me even though we were poor.

But the label "poverty" had not yet been invented or applied to people like my family. We thought we were fortunate to have three meals a day, a change of overalls and cheap tennis shoes to wear. Those shoes cost 89 cents, and a shirt and pair of pants were less than a dollar. We didn't have much money, but things were cheap. I'm glad the government didn't classify us at poverty level because I felt fine about our situation.

As fall ebbed toward the Christmas season, I began to yearn for the pretty bicycle I kept admiring in the hardware store. If I could entice Santa to bring me that bike, I could pedal up and down the road to see my friends.

I made certain that my folks realized I absolutely had to have that bike for Christmas. While we were in town one Saturday just before Christmas, I showed Dad my dream cycle. "With that bike I could ride all over the farm,"

I said. "I could drive the cows in from the pasture for milking, and there are a thousand other ways I could use that bike to help out on the farm."

But Dad was no fool. "The Dust Bowl is killing us, son," he explained, "and the New Deal has run the price of cotton down to 5 cents. Grain is worthless. The Depression has the entire nation on its knees."

"I've been on my knees all fall dragging a heavy cotton sack," I replied, "and I hoed a thousand rows of cotton and maize during the summer. Think of how many maize heads I cut and tossed into the wagon. I help milk the cows, feed the pigs and take care of the chickens."

He backed off a little. "I know, son. You've done a lot of work on the farm, and I appreciate what you do. But a new bike costs a mint of money for poor folks."

"I've *gotta* have that bike," I told him. "Santa knows that I need it and would use it every day."

"Well now," he said, stalling, "this Dust Bowl and the Depression have hit old Santa hard. He may not have toys to deliver this Christmas."

"Just so he brings me that bike," I said.

Then it happened. Five days before Christmas, a cold wind blew in from the north. When I came in from helping milk our cows, Mother said, "I think we are going to have a blue norther."

I shivered. "It's really getting cold," I said.

No one liked what the old-timers called blue northers. The sky would turn deep blue in the north and the wind would tear down across the plains all the way from Canada. Temperatures would plunge, water pipes would freeze, and life would be miserable in the zero-degree weather.

But this storm turned out to be something more than a blue norther. The wind was stronger by noon; then clouds began drifting across the sky. When we did the milking and feeding that night, I realized just how cold the flat plains could get. The wind was hitting 40 miles

Twenty-seven people had come to our house for shelter, crowding our home in search of warmth.
With so many people to feed, Mother began cooking the things we had canned to get by on during the winter.

an hour, and the temperature had dropped from 35 degrees in the early morning to only 8 degrees by nightfall. Thirty minutes outside was enough to freeze a person unless he was wearing lots of clothes.

The house was cold even though Mother had fires burning in the stoves. Our unheated bedrooms were like ice. The bitter cold seeped through the old walls, chilling everyone.

When Dad came in from feeding the mules, he warmed for a minute by the stove. "I'm glad we have those six sacks of coal and the wood under the shed," he said. "I'm afraid this will be a real spell."

How right he was! When we awoke the next morning, snow was beginning to fall and the wind was hitting 50 miles an hour. Dad got the stove burning as hot as it could stand, and the room was *still* cool. "It must be below zero," he said. "We'll hurry with breakfast and get out there to care for the stock."

School had let out for Christmas, so we did not have to worry about getting there. But taking care of the stock was chore enough. Dad tuned the radio to Amarillo. The announcer cautioned that it was below zero; the winds were expected to strengthen during the day and snow was anticipated. "Stay inside and do not attempt to travel, as snow will drift and close many roads," he warned.

A breakfast of hot biscuits, gravy and scrambled eggs warmed us for the cold task ahead. Even so, tending to our morning chores was a challenge. Our hands froze stiff as we tried to milk the cows under the open shed. The ice on the surface of the stock tank was 2 inches thick. Dad had to swing an ax with all his might to break it so we could water the cows.

In the midst of that bitterly cold snow and wind, I kept thinking about riding my new bike on warm spring days. Life then would be grand!

But things turned sour for my family.

The storm intensified as the day progressed.

We watched a few cars bounce along the dirt highway near our home; they all struggled to make it through the storm.

That afternoon, a car hit a snowdrift near our house. It bounced and lurched before becoming hopelessly stuck across the middle of the road. The highway crews could do no good in the high wind. A few moments later, another car got stuck trying to get around the first car. We watched as the men pushed and heaved, trying to get a car through the drift, but the old machines could not make it.

As we were preparing to do our evening milking and tend to the livestock, the two families walked to our house, carrying the younger children. They were half-frozen and the kids were crying. They did not get a chance to ask if they could come in; Mother and Dad met them on the porch and helped them get inside, out of the blizzard.

My family was never one to refuse help to someone in need. Mother invited them happily. "You folks come on in and stay with us until the weather breaks." So we had nine visitors that we did not need.

Dad, my brother and I hurried out to do the evening chores in the height of the storm. When we returned some 40 minutes later, we found two more families who had walked to the house from their abandoned automobiles. The roads were impassable, and the wind and snow continued.

Mother and Sister had begun cooking when we went out to do the chores, and they were still cooking and feeding people until after 9 p.m. Two other families with children walked to the house to avoid freezing to death in their cars.

Twenty-seven people had come to our house for shelter, crowding our home in search of warmth. Bedtime was a disaster. We had only 2½ beds, not enough for even the babies. The folks left our fires burning through the night, trying to get some heat into the bedrooms for the children. People slept in their clothes, using what few quilts and blankets we had. The men fed the stove throughout the frozen night.

With so many people to feed, Mother began cooking the things we had canned to get by on during the winter. As I watched our little supply of food dwindle rapidly, I knew all hope of getting that pretty bike was gone. Survival was all that mattered now.

The storm did not abate the next day, so the people had to stay with us. Mother and the other ladies cooked all day, trying to feed 32 people.

I was so tired that second night that I tried to curl up in an old quilt and sleep behind the stove. As I lay on the cold floor, I prayed, "Dear God, please make this storm cease so that these people can get on their way. I know I won't get any presents, but if the storm ceases, I'll be happy. Amen."

When we woke the next morning, it seemed that a miracle had taken place. A gentle southwestern wind was bringing warmer air into the area. The sun peeped over the horizon and the terrible storm was broken.

By noon water was beginning to drip from the roof as the snow began to melt. The men took shovels and went to dig their cars out of the big drift. Highway graders came along and opened the road.

Before long, all our guests had left. To my surprise, they had taken up a collection to help pay for the food they had eaten. Mother had $36.40. It was not nearly enough to pay for all the food, but it was a generous gift from poor folks.

On Christmas Eve I went to sleep in my own bed with my older brother. I was happy even though I had given up on my bicycle. Just having our home to ourselves seemed like a real Christmas treat. Of course, I was happy that we had probably saved some lives during the blizzard.

Dad had to call me to wake me in that cold room on Christmas morning. I struggled into my clothes, then walked into the living room. There I received the shock of my life. Unbelievable as it seemed, there stood my beautiful blue-and-white bicycle! I don't know how the folks managed it, but it was the grandest thing that ever happened to me. Brother and Sister also got what they wanted from Santa.

What had seemed so tragic for three days turned out to be the most wonderful Christmas ever. ❖

Cob Fighting

By Merle Nickell

When teenage boys get together, you can be fairly certain they will find a way to amuse themselves. City or country, summer or winter, good times or bad, it makes no difference. They can be found doing something exciting and, more often than not, a little dangerous. We forget, sometimes, that only a short time ago, they were children and that they still possess the vivid imaginations and sense of adventure that dominated their childhood.

I went through that fascinating period of life in the late 1930s through the early 1940s. In those days, very little money trickled down to the teenage population, and automobiles were scarce enough that it was no problem for most people in the county to match them with their respective owners. With no cars and practically no money, what did we do for excitement? Lots of things, but let me tell you about just one of them—cob fighting.

But not just any corncob would satisfy a skillful cob fighter, and he selected each with care. In order to throw them straight, he would break them at just the right place.

Before World War II, West Liberty, Ky., was one of those small towns that had yet to ban barns within the city limits. Luckily for the boys who loved to cob fight, some of these barns made excellent "forts." The ideal ones had a loft over the stalls and were a little on the dilapidated side, with a few boards missing here and there.

There were several ways to organize a good cob fight. Probably the most popular one was for a gang of boys to divide into two groups, with one defending and the other attacking the fort. Before the battle began, each side would spend a few minutes stockpiling corncobs. They were plentiful in every barnyard, and they served as the only ammunition.

But not just any corncob would satisfy a skillful cob fighter, and he selected each with care. In order to throw them straight, he would break them at just the right place. If they were too long or too light at one end, they had a tendency to curve in flight and served no useful purpose.

The heavy artillery consisted of large, wet corncobs that had been lying in the barnyard for some time. It probably goes without saying that it was not just the rainwater that made them wet and soggy.

The objective of the attacking army, of course, was to take the fort. Once the battle began, the rules were simple. If a combatant was hit by a cob, he was "dead" and must sit out the rest of the fight.

The outcome depended largely on the strategy employed by each side. Sometimes the attackers simultaneously rushed the fort from all sides. But that was pretty risky business and usually wasn't tried until several of the defenders had been eliminated.

Slipping into a stall through a gap left by a missing board was a favorite and often-used tactic. Once the attackers got into the stalls, they could usually force the defenders who were stationed on the ground level back up into the loft. It was a great thrill to dash from a stall into the hallway, exchange a few volleys with the enemy overhead, and then duck back into the safety of the stall.

Sometimes the defenders used an offensive tactic of their own. For instance, at a given signal a certain number of them would jump out of the loft and fight the attackers in the open or charge them from the rear.

Certainly one of the attractions of a cob fight was the opportunity to display a variety of skills. Some boys were extremely agile and hard to hit, even at close range. Others possessed strong and accurate throwing arms that immediately attracted everyone's attention. Some boys exhibited a certain amount of derring-do and were extremely effective fighters, even though they lacked the agility or strong throwing arms of some of their comrades. Then there were the natural leaders, who were offered the opportunity to formulate strategy and lead their men into battle.

As I look back on those days, I can recognize another important feature of cob fighting. It was a comparatively safe pastime, even though an element of danger was always present. I cannot recall one incident where a boy was seriously hurt. In my own career as a cob fighter, I remember sustaining only one injury that amounted to more than a temporary sting. I had slipped into a stall with the intention of jumping out into the hallway for a few good potshots at the enemy in the loft. However, my entry into the stall had not gone unnoticed. My brother, Lynn, spotted me from above, and he knew exactly what I had in mind. He quickly slipped down the ladder into the hallway and waited for me to make my move. He was armed with one of those heavy, wet cobs, and when I stuck my head out in to the hallway—whamo!—right in the mouth! For the next few days, two fat lips bore testimony as to how I fared in that battle.

The lifestyle of teenage boys has changed drastically since those days. I would not attempt to weigh one against the other, but it doesn't hurt to reminisce a little. Even though it is impossible to turn back the clock, I have a sneaking suspicion that today's teenage boys would enjoy a cob fight just as much as we did. ❖

Political Picnics

By Forrest S. Clark

My mother and father didn't always have enough food for the family and times were hard. My father had been unemployed for some time. The year was 1935.

It was the custom in those times for politicians to give gigantic outdoor political rallies and picnics and invite thousands from the cities to go out for a day in the country. This was a way to get a day's outing, but it also was a way to get a free dinner or lunch for the entire family.

One day we all went down and caught the train. It was loaded with other families, all bound for the great picnic to be held in Sea Girt, N.J., on the grounds of the governor's mansion and summer home at the seashore.

Train after train carried city folk to the vast picnic grounds. It was a hot midsummer day with the temperature near 90 degrees.

As we stepped down from the train, each of us was handed a huge box lunch and directed to a certain area of the picnic grounds. I remember how happy we were to be outside and enjoy a bountiful meal.

There must have been 30,000 people there, including most of the highest-ranking state officials. One or two climbed on top of an old Ford and started making speeches.

A large brass band played all the popular patriotic songs, including many Sousa marches that were favorites in the 1930s. At the very moment they played *Stars and Stripes Forever*, a contingent of U.S. Army soldiers marched onto the field. That was impressive.

The dust rose over the crowd all dressed in white. The heat bore down, and far off one could hear the ocean on the shoreline. At 13, I had never before seen such a large crowd in one place. The men all wore straw hats and the women wore bonnets to shield them from the midday sun.

As the sun began to go down, we boarded the trains again and left that place of dreams. Thus ended one of the outstanding days of my childhood during the Great Depression. ❖

House Parties

By Mrs. Thomas Zahno

*A*nyone remember the Good Old Days of house parties during the Depression of the late 1920s and early 1930s? What fun we had during those "depressing" times!

Mom, Dad and my kid brother would play for round and square dances at house parties, weddings, etc., to keep our family going financially. Mom could play almost any musical instrument—accordion, piano, guitar. Dad played the violin, and my brother, the drum or guitar. Mom could hear a piece of music once or twice and memorize it. They all played "by ear" and were in great demand in those days.

One lovely group of neighbors and friends would go from one person's house on one Friday night to another house the following Friday night. They would play progressive 500—a card game—for a couple of hours, then award an inexpensive first prize for the highest score and a comical booby prize for the lowest.

Around 10 o'clock, the rugs were rolled back, furniture moved around and the dancing would begin. Usually, we had no professional caller; we knew the calls and would call them ourselves as we danced, like this one, sung to the tune of *Nellie Gray*:

Oh, it's allemande left with the lady on the left,
Give your right hand to your partner
And it's grand right and left.
When you're halfway around,
You promenade her home
And you all swing your darling Nellie Gray!

There were the round dances, the foxtrots, waltzes, quadrilles and polkas.

Usually after a three-part square dance, the musicians would have a five-minute break to rest. Playing through three sets of square dances was strenuous, especially pulling that accordion back and forth.

At midnight there was a break for refreshments. How good the coffee smelled! The hostess for the evening made large kettles of it with the fresh grounds tied up in a cloth bag. No luxuries back then like 30-cup coffee makers! Everyone brought sandwiches packed in a shoebox. These were all mixed together and passed around on plates. We often sat on the floor to eat, leaning against the wall.

Children of all sizes attended these parties, too. Who could afford baby-sitters—and who wanted them? When they couldn't stay awake any longer, they were put to bed among the piles of coats on the beds.

After the midnight snack was cleared away, it was more dancing—usually until 3 o'clock. I remember my folks would usually start playing *It's Three O'Clock in the Morning*, then follow with *Home Sweet Home*. For this grueling evening's work, they usually received the handsome sum of $3. Everyone hated to break up the evening's fun! On more than one occasion they would ask the folks if they would play longer. Although dead tired, they usually agreed. Then someone would pass the hat for a free-will collection of dimes, quarters or whatever families could afford. Everyone was happy for the extra hour of enjoyment, and my parents would have another dollar or a dollar and a quarter.

My parents also played every Saturday night for a different group. The Saturday-night group was a rough-and-ready, "hard cider" type. Everyone usually had a good time, too, even though a couple of the fellows sometimes would have a little too much and go outside for a black eye or bloody nose. I was always terrified, but nothing more serious ever developed out of it. Sometimes this group also took up the collection for an extra hour of fun.

One time during a blizzard, my parents played until dawn. It was lucky Mom could play the guitar, too, as her arms wouldn't play the accordion any longer. After having some

Swing Your Partner by Jay Killian, House of White Birches nostalgia archives

car trouble with their old Model T, they finally arrived back home just as people were going to church.

Then there were the good old family parties! We were of German descent and sometimes at a birthday, wedding or anniversary, our parents would again be the musicians. They never had a chance to dance and enjoy themselves, but they were quite amused, just the same, by some of the antics on the dance floor.

At these parties the old German folk dances were often requested. I remember the Herr Schmidt, a dance with a partner. You would face each other toe-to-toe, shuffle your feet back and forth with a slight hop, and then, when the music changed, sort of waltz around the room until the tempo changed to the toe-to-toe part again. Then there was the Rhinelander and the schottische (almost like a polka).

There aren't many of the older people left that used to go to these parties. Isn't it strange, with all our comforts and conveniences, that we can look back on those Depression days with nostalgia—even longing? ❖

Shopping for Clothes

By Mildred Loehr

The Saturday before school started in Kansas City back in the Good Old Days was always a red-letter event, for this was one of the few times during the year when we bought new clothes. This was a necessity since our school clothes from last year were outgrown, faded and worn, and last year's shoes were too small for feet that had roamed barefoot all summer. Daddy always found a screen door to fix or some yard work to do on this day. Shopping for girls' clothes was strictly women's work.

As we walked into our nearby Sears, Roebuck and Co. store, we felt a proprietary interest. Each change in floor arrangement and displays was duly noted and commented upon. The escalator in the middle of the building was a roundabout way to the second floor and the girls' and women's wear, but no visit to Sears would have been complete without a trip on this marvelous invention. Besides, at the top of the escalator was the ladies' restroom, with its lighted mirrors and overstuffed chairs. They were a delight—almost as pretty as some of the ornate bathrooms we saw on the movie screen.

The two dresses we selected would have to last an entire school year, so they must be durable, large enough to "grow into" and colorful, since they would fade soon enough from repeated scrubbings on the washboard.

While my mother and older sister looked through racks of dresses for the most stylish clothes at bargain prices, I retreated to my private fantasyland. The ladies' department boasted a full-length mirror flanked on each side by a hinged mirror. By folding these together I made a triangular alcove where I was concealed from view except for my legs and feet. (Like the ostrich, I blissfully ignored that small detail.) There I danced and dreamed the minutes away. I was Ginger Rogers dancing with Fred Astaire; I was Irene Castle dancing with Vernon Castle; I was Sonja Henie ice-skating at Winter Carnival; I was Judy Garland, Carmen Miranda, Mae West. The magical mirror reflected not a skinny little girl with pipestem arms, skinned knees and dirty fingernails but a lovely, voluptuous woman clothed in satin, sequins and pearls, with furs around my neck. I was almost sorry to hear my mother say, "C'mon, Honey. Let's go get your things now."

My sister was a beautiful girl and clothes seemed to fit her to perfection. What a letdown when *I* started trying on dresses! The two dresses we selected would have to last an entire school year, so they must be durable, large enough to "grow into" and colorful, since they would fade soon enough from repeated scrubbings on the washboard.

Since my mother always optimistically over-estimated my rate of growth, most of the time I looked like a stick figure with a dress draped on it. It never occurred to me to object; I think I felt it was my fault for not growing faster. And after all, it was fun to wear something that smelled and looked brand-new.

The lingerie department was the next stop. I was permitted to choose two pairs of real silk panties from a collection of apricot, peach, baby blue, pink and white. This was a difficult decision, and to this day I collect lovely underwear as some women do shoes—one more pair isn't too many and 10 pairs aren't enough. Two cotton undershirts were bought at maternal insistence— I just *knew* Mae West didn't wear undershirts.

Later we bought another hated item: long, brown, cotton stockings and enough elastic to make two pairs of garters. These stockings had special qualities that enabled them to sag at knee, midcalf and ankle and slide down into my shoes just 30 seconds after being tugged tight.

Two pairs of anklets completed the sale, and we moved on to the shoe department.

Shoes were serious business. My mother suffered greatly from corns, bunions and ingrown toenails, which she felt were the result of poorly fitting shoes. In hopes of sparing me the same trouble, each pair was thoroughly examined, punched, probed and finally fluoroscoped while I was wearing them to assure proper fit. The name Buster Brown or Red Goose adorned the inside of each shoe. In spite of all these precautions, quite often I had to stuff cotton in the toes, and it was a sure bet the first day of school would leave me with at least one blister.

With all shopping out of the way, we finally made our way to the lunch counter. With packages piled around us, we enjoyed a plate lunch and iced tea, tired but happy. Not one of those packages contained anything for my mother, but she never mentioned that. In fact, the thought only occurs to me as I write this.

About the first of November we shopped for winter wear. Snow pants, much like those now worn for skiing, were worn with a matching jacket similar to a car coat. Made of heavy wool and lined with cotton batting and an inner lining, they made us look like clumsy teddy bears when we wore them. Wool hats and mittens and

buckle galoshes completed the ensemble, which protected us from the most severe weather. I envied one girl who had a very stylish snowsuit with a flared, full-length top and a real beaver collar, muff and hat.

We shopped for clothes at only one other time of year—Easter. For this occasion, we boarded a streetcar and rode to downtown Kansas City. Alighting at 12th and Main, we walked north, past the exclusive shops, past the large department stores, out of the high-rent district, to a store at Sixth and Main whose name has intrigued my children and grandchildren as it did me: Store Without a Name. Like the concept of infinity, the notion of a store whose name was no name fascinated me.

There I picked out a stiff taffeta dress that wrinkled if I sat down in it, a shapeless slip, new underpants, white anklets and, with due care, a pair of white shoes. A straw bonnet, a purse and a silk parasol made in Japan and decorated with hand-painted flowers completed my ensemble. On Easter Sunday I would parade like a peacock in my new finery. I would come home with new blisters on my feet, legs scratched from the taffeta dress and ears irritated by the straw hat— but that was a small price to pay for such elegance! ❖

Better Than a Silver Spoon

By Betty Artlip Lawson

One is indeed fortunate if memories of one's childhood call to mind more times of laughter than times of sorrow. It is my great good luck to be able to say I may count myself as one of this fortunate group.

I was most certainly *not* "born with a silver spoon in my mouth." Indeed, few assets of any sort belonged to the family into which I was born in 1931. My arrival brought a fifth child into an already full house.

But we had something in our home that more than made up for the lack of material things. My brothers and sisters and I had the great good fortune to be members of a household where "proper parents" were in charge.

These very fine parents had the power to make us laugh when we thought we wished to cry. They were possessed of a magic that caused us to forget the discomfort of extreme cold and miserable heat—and we experienced plenty of both in Iowa. These two fine adults had the power to help us be proud of wearing patched, faded clothing. Their special abilities allowed our dear parents to keep from us children the knowledge that our family was considered by others to be "poor."

Our house might not have been as warm in temperature as some of our more prosperous neighbors, but we soon forgot the cold in the efforts of our taffy pulls.

I knew of poor families. These had a father who was addicted to drink and/or punished children severely. Perhaps these poor families were cursed with a mother who was considered shiftless and seemed forever angry with her children. These mothers might let their children go hungry or dirty—perhaps hungry *and* dirty in the very poorest families.

But my family most surely wasn't in this category. My dad did not drink, swear or administer any kind of physical punishment. He didn't make much money when we were growing up, but he loved us and was very good to us. Our good fortune knew no bounds, for besides this very good father, we were blessed with a mother with a marvelous outlook on life. She made us laugh, she played with us and she never gave us reason to doubt her love for us or her ability to care for us. She worked hard, laughed at her troubles and never let us suspect that we were considered poor in the eyes of some.

Mother saved thin cardboard and made us a deck of cards. We children learned rummy, hearts, fish and all the other games we were able to learn. Children from all over our end of town came to play with our homemade deck of cards. They might have had factory-made cards at home, but they didn't have our mother who made the games so exciting.

The sweet treats that came our way were shared with all who were in our home. Many winter evenings, our already overcrowded 3½-room house would come alive with neighborhood children. Our house might not have been as warm in temperature as some of our more prosperous neighbors, but we soon forgot the cold in the efforts of our taffy pulls. In our house you were never warned to be careful or quiet. We ate every bite of the taffy, once it was sufficiently plastered onto us and some of our surroundings. We were required to clean up ourselves before going to bed, but by the time we returned from school the following day, the rest of the messy evidence had vanished. Once again our small, underfurnished home was spotless and ready for any and all action suggested by one of us five half-grown children and our baby brother.

I shudder to think just how hectic our mother's days must have been. Yet she never seemed tired and was always ready for a game of cards, checkers or whatever presented itself. It was her way of life. She spent her free hours during the day in an all-out effort to make for us a childhood to remember.

My family never accepted government commodities as did many of our neighbors. I can remember how, as a very young child, my mouth would salivate at the sight of a child with a welfare orange. But we knew that the very evening of the day of the commodity release, we would get one of our mom's special treats for an after-dinner snack. It might be only popcorn balls made with sorghum, but to us it seemed food fine enough for the angels.

We grew up sturdy and strong. We might have been denied creature comforts, but we never lacked the all-important

love and security of a happy home. And we were among the most fortunate to have been blessed with parents who did not question the importance of these two things, but set about providing them for us to the best of their ability.

Dad passed away in 1972 at the age of 78. He was proud of his six honest, hardworking offspring, and we never gave him cause to be ashamed of any of us. We knew what having a father of his caliber was worth and we were more than pleased with him.

Mom was as good a grandmother and great-grandmother as she was a mother. She was a favorite of all her grandchildren and she allowed them to use her house as they please, just as she did with us.

To say that this woman was beloved is a gross understatement. She was one of the most remarkable human beings I ever knew, and there are at least five others who share my opinion. To that number should be added her 11 grandchildren and the two great-grandchildren who had the good fortune to know her well. The other great-grandchildren can always take their parents' and grandparents' word for it:

No, we never thought of ourselves as poor. We could never be poor with such wonderful parents. ❖

1932 Campbell's Soup Ad, House of White Birches nostalgia archives

© *Memories* by Jim Daly

Making Ends Meet

Chapter 5

I know that when it came to making ends meet, Mama was a master. She could make a meal seemingly out of thin air. Her penchant at using and reusing fabric from mercantile bolt to rag bin was legendary. String from feed sacks was judiciously saved, wound tightly into a large ball and kept against the day when we might need it.

To me, Mama's expertise at making ends meet was best illustrated at the schoolhouse. There was always something nutritious in my pail—a big task for a young woman with three pails to pack each day. "An apple a day keeps the doctor away," she said, as she crowned lunches with a pome from the cellar. She knew how important it was to keep the doctor away.

School clothes were always a challenge, since shoes, shirts, socks and pants needed to last a year (before the recycling efforts began). Mama was an excellent seamstress. She augmented Daddy's earnings by sewing for folks, and everyone agreed she was one of the best around. So Mama made our Christmas presents. When we looked under the tree Christmas morning there was a beautiful dress for my little sister, a suit of clothes for my big brother and a winter coat, made from pale green corduroy material, for me.

Wow! That coat was as good as any, for any price, from any catalog I ever looked through. Mama had lined it to turn the winter wind. There was a deep collar that could be turned up under a scarf for even greater insulation. All during the Christmas and New Year's holiday season I wore my new coat proudly.

Then came the first day back at school (I was 11 and a big fifth grader). Of course, I wore Mama's gift proudly into the classroom, stopping to hang it on a peg at the back. As I did, one of my more sophisticated classmates noted there was no manufacturer's tag in the coat. "What?" he guffawed, "Is that thing *homemade*? (He spit it out like an epithet.) My mom only buys me store-bought coats." After having my prized present ridiculed, I spent the rest of the day in torment, not knowing whether to be proud or ashamed. As the day ended, I pulled on my coat and stepped out of the schoolhouse and into the north wind. The icy chill of the winter day blew some common sense back into my young head.

My coat was made with something a store-bought coat never could have: Mama's love. In love Mama had made ends meet while giving me as good a coat as any store-bought one. That was nothing to be ashamed about.

As I neared our home, my head went up and my chest went out; I warmly walked in wearing the best Christmas gift a boy could hope for. And the next day I straightened out that sophisticated classmate.

—*Ken Tate*

© *A Perfect Pair* by John Sloane

From Pumpkins to High-Buttoned Shoes

By Evalyn Pflueger

*L*ast evening when I opened our local newspaper and saw the front-page picture of a huge pumpkin patch, my mind leaped back to the story of the pumpkins and the high-buttoned shoes.

In the Jack Pine Plains of Lower Michigan, the soil is so sandy that rain immediately drains deep into the ground, leaving very little to nourish the vegetation. Because of this, about the only things that grow there are scrub oaks and a stunted variety of tree called jack pine. This region is sparsely settled by people who try to eke out a living by farming.

When I was a little girl, my father was a dentist in a small town near the Jack Pine Plains. Many of the children in our school walked the mile or two to get to our school. Millie Banks was one of these children. But every day, come rain, shine or deep snow, Millie was there in her seat, ready for the day before the last bell rang called us in from the playground.

I felt sorry for Millie. Her dresses reached almost to her ankles. She never wore big bows of ribbon in her hair like the rest of us. Her hair was parted in the middle, plaited into two severe braids, and tied with string saved from packages brought from the general store. But worst of all were those heavy shoes she wore—brogans, they were called.

We all knew that she had to wear durable shoes; nice leather ones like the shoes we town children wore wouldn't last long for a child walking a mile-and-a-half back and forth to school each day. But that didn't help, and those heavy shoes seemed cruel punishment for Millie. She never said anything, but day after day, she sat in class with her feet folded as far back under her chair as she could get them, trying to make them as inconspicuous as possible.

Millie passed my house on her way back and forth to town, so it was quite natural that we would walk home from school together as far as my house. We soon became close friends. There was something so solid and sensible about her that pulled me to her. In fact, she was well liked at school. During our playground games, she never cried or got mad as some of the girls did when the games got rough. And Millie got the best grades in the class, so she was also popular with the teachers.

One day as we were walking through town on our way home from school, admiring things in the store windows, Millie stopped squarely in front of a pair of shoes in Morton's Shoe Store. "I'm going to have a pair of shoes just like that," she declared.

Now, I knew that was impossible, even if Millie didn't. My mother had told me how hard it was for the Bankses; Mr. Banks was not a strong man, so much of the farm work fell on Mrs. Banks. She had her chickens and cow to care for, besides helping with the work in the fields. Money was too dear for them to spend it on impractical clothes.

But there, in all their glory, stood the shoes. They were wonderful—black, button-up shoes, almost knee high, crowned by the *pièce de résistance,* a strip of red patent leather around the top with a tassel hanging down the side. It was the most beautiful pair of shoes either of us had ever seen.

"You know, Millie, you can never have a pair of shoes like that," I reminded her. "They would wear out in no time walking to school like you do."

"I don't care. I'm going to get them," she stubbornly replied. "I'll carry them in my book bag and change when I get to school."

"What will you buy them with?" Nine-year-old girls can be very practical, especially when they are trying to talk their friends out of something they would like for themselves. But sometimes poor little farm girls were undeterred when deciding on ways to make ends meet.

"I'll raise … pumpkins? Yes, I'll raise pumpkins!"

Pumpkins had just popped into her head, and I could tell she was as surprised as I. Whoever heard of a little girl raising pumpkins to buy a pair of shoes?

"But that would take a whole year," I objected. "The shoes will be sold by then."

"There will be shoes like that next year," Millie replied confidently. "I can plant my seed next spring and next fall I will have new, high-buttoned shoes. You just see!"

"With a red top band and tassel?" I had to ask.

"With a red top band and tassel," she declared, and she emphasized it with a stamp of her foot.

We started on up the street. Soon I had forgotten the shoes—but I was reminded of them again the next afternoon, and the next, and the next. Every day we had to stop and admire those shoes on the way home, and every day Millie was more determined to have shoes just like them.

Before we knew it, school was out for the summer. At least once a week, Millie came in to visit me or I went out to her house. One day when I went to visit her, Millie took me to the field beside the house to show me the little pumpkin plants that were just showing their heads out of the ground. I could tell from her expression that Millie wasn't seeing pumpkin sprouts; she was seeing high-buttoned shoes with red bands and tassels.

From then on, we didn't play when I was at Millie's. We spent our time on our knees, weeding pumpkins.

"I declare, you girls are getting calluses on your knees," Millie's father teased.

"You'll have to walk with books on your heads all winter to get straightened up again," her mother remarked.

Finally the little pumpkins began to form. It was fun walking around the patch each morning, counting each new little green ball that would soon be a big yellow pumpkin. We called them pumpkinettes. By now, we were all excited about Millie's project—even my mother and father. Everything was developing according to Millie's plans.

Then, one morning when I was almost at Millie's gate, she came running out to meet me. Her eyes were red and swollen from crying.

"What's happened?" I exclaimed.

"Something came in the night and ate every one of my little pumpkinettes." Millie was crying again. "And now I won't have my beautiful shoes."

"Won't there be any more pumpkinettes formed?"

"Yes, but I need every one," she lamented.

"Let's go see." I was almost as upset as Millie.

When we got to the field, Mr. Banks was walking around the patch like a hound on a scent. "Yes, it's just what I thought," he announced as he came up to us. "Mother coon and her little ones had a good feed on your pumpkins last night."

"What can we do now? Are all of them gone? I don't think this is fair," I remonstrated.

"This is farming," he answered. "Things like this happen every year. You just think you're going to have a good year and maybe get out of debt, and then here comes a rain and washes everything out, or there's a drought and everything dries up, or there's a hailstorm. And now this." I wondered if he was going to sit down and cry, too.

"Well, let's see what we can do," he finally said. "It's early, and there are lots of blossoms left. If we can keep the coons out, you should have a good crop yet."

But here was another problem. How do you keep raccoons out of a pumpkin patch at night? It didn't take Millie long to decide. She would sleep there the rest of the summer—and of course, I said I'd sleep with her. We had an old camping cot and Millie took the bedding from her bed and we moved to the pumpkin patch. At first we had trouble making Millie's dog realize that he was to guard the patch with us, but finally he became used to being tied to the foot of the cot.

What an adventure it was! We were practically right outside Mr. and Mrs. Banks' bedroom window, but we felt like we were way out in the wilds. When Spot would wake us with his barking, Millie would untie him and away he would go, chasing intruders out of the field. The nights were balmy. Sometimes we'd get up, walk all around the patch, and then go back to bed. Spot soon learned to settle down beside us without being tied.

Pumpkins had just popped into her head, and I could tell she was as surprised as I. Whoever heard of a little girl raising pumpkins to buy a pair of shoes.

The pumpkins grew and the summer wore on. We hadn't had intruders for weeks, and now it was time for school to start. I had to move home. The weeding and watching were over. We could hardly wait for the harvesting in October.

By now, Millie's project had become the interest of the whole town. Mr. Lowery, the editor of our weekly paper, had printed an article about it. He also suggested to Millie's father that when they were ready to sell, Millie could bring in a wagonload and tie the horses in front of the newspaper office in the middle of town to sell them. My father said it was so he could keep track of the sales and write a success story afterward.

One Friday while she was in school, Millie's parents loaded the wagon with the plump yellow and orange jewels. The next day, bright and early, Millie came riding to town all alone, proudly sitting on the board seat, holding the reins high over the horses' rumps. That is, she was alone until she got to my house. I was to enjoy the fun of selling pumpkins, too.

I'll swear, every mother in town brought her children down to the wagon to buy their jack-o'-lantern pumpkins. And I'll bet there were more pumpkins eaten that year in Marion, Mich., than any year before or since. My father finally complained that pumpkin pie was coming out of his ears.

We sold them all and Millie got her new shoes—*and* her first store-bought dress with a hair ribbon to match. This would be one dress that wasn't too long; my mother saw to that. And she had a good excuse for shortening it: We were to have our picture taken by the empty wagon for Mr. Lowery's follow-up story. Naturally Millie had to be decked out in her new clothes.

That winter, it was a common sight to see a group of beaming fourth-graders gathered around Millie, helping her shed her "walking shoes" for the high-top buttoned shoes with the red patent leather tops and the tassels hanging down the sides. ❖

The Wardrobe Conspiracy

By Laverne Shirley

I have always loved conspiracy. I've been involved in several—none more exciting and rewarding than one when I was about 9 years old, during the dark Depression days of the 1930s. That's when I joined forces with Mama to outwit Daddy to buy a wardrobe.

In all ways I was Daddy's girl and very defensive about him. But this time I believed him to be a stubborn tightwad. It did not trouble my conscience, therefore, to be a turncoat.

The problem really began several years before I was born. When my parents were building our two-story stone house, Daddy instructed the stonemason that no windows were to be put in the north wall, so the house would be warmer in winter. Mama was appalled, but her pleading—and eventually, her bullying—did not deter him from this windowless idiosyncrasy. She appealed to the stonemason who agreed with her that the house would be a monstrosity with a tall, blank wall.

After years of complaining about the lack of closets, Mama drove nails in adjoining walls and strung a wire from them across a corner.

He began teasing Daddy about the house resembling an institution and how strangers would be asking what prison or asylum it was. Daddy finally relented and allowed four windows in the wall, but he would not allow the carpenters to construct a closet in any of the four bedrooms. The only closet was under the stairs. It opened into the kitchen, making it an excellent storage spot for canned fruits and vegetables—but not for clothes.

Our clothes lay folded inside dresser drawers. Starched dresses were laid carefully across the sewing machine. Shoes stood in a row beneath the dresser. Off-season clothes were stored in boxes under beds.

After years of complaining about the lack of closets, Mama drove nails in adjoining walls and strung a wire from them across a corner. Our dresses and Daddy's suit were hung behind a flowered cretonne curtain. But she sighed in exasperation at the tacky structure and vowed that she was going to have a closet in every bedroom someday.

The Montgomery Ward catalog came to her rescue. On its furniture pages she found a wardrobe for $39.99. Her mind began working like well-oiled cogwheels as she worked out a plan to get the money. Cash was as scarce as the proverbial pot of gold at the end of the rainbow; but Mama figured out a scheme.

She rounded up a dozen of the best milkers among Daddy's cows, bought a cream separator on credit, and began shipping cream. Knowing that he didn't want his calves stunted, she promised Daddy she'd milk only half of each cow's udder. Poor Daddy thought Mama was trying to help him pay taxes and hired hands.

Seeing how much she was making from those cows, she rounded up eight or 10 more, hired two neighbor girls by paying them a lard bucket of milk each day, and shipped *more* cream. She envisioned the wardrobe arriving in a couple of months.

Washing the separator utensils became my job. I detested the task, but I wanted that wardrobe as badly as Mama did.

Extra vegetables and fruits were sold to a woman with a restaurant. Eggs were hunted in all the nooks where hens might hide a nest. Then I washed them and they were packed in egg crates to be sold weekly in town. And our fryers ended up not on our own table, smothered in dumplings, but on the restaurant tables to feed traveling salesmen.

Mama raked up money from every source she could think. The angel-food cake pan on the top shelf of the cabinet grew heavier each week with coins and bills. The wardrobe was practically in our downstairs bedroom.

But Daddy shoved it out of our house, down the road and back into a Kansas City warehouse by asking Mama for $30 to pay his hired hands. With a white, crestfallen face, Mama stared at him.

"You have been saving the cream and egg money, haven't you?" he asked.

"Yes," Mama replied lamely. She went to the kitchen and brought out the cake pan, counted out the money and gave a deep sigh of resignation.

"Mama," I pleaded, "why did you give him our money?"

"I thought how the hired men have been working for your daddy to feed their families," she told me.

We started again with a few dollars, milked more cows and sold more eggs. The cake pan began to fill again and our spirits lifted.

Then they hit the depths of a bottomless pit when Daddy came asking for money to pay the men for threshing our wheat. Our debts must be paid, for Daddy didn't believe in owing anyone money; neither did Mama. With slower steps than before, she brought the cake pan and counted the money into Daddy's hand.

Mama despaired for weeks. I cried and fumed in resentment that my family was poor and times were hard. Fruit and vegetable season was past, the chickens laid few eggs and the cows were turned out into the stalk fields to forage. There was no opportunity now for Mama and me to make money. The few dollars remaining in the cake pan stayed put until it was time to bake the Christmas fruitcake.

In the meantime, summer clothes went under the bed. Winter clothes hung behind the cretonne curtain, and coats were laid over the back of an old rocking chair. But Mama wasn't out—she was just down for the winter.

When spring came, the cows were put into the pasture and thick yellow cream poured from the separator spout again. The hens laid hundreds of eggs—at least it seemed so to me—and flocks of tiny red chicks scratched in the barnyard, waiting for their day on the restaurant table. Green beans in the garden were increased from two rows to four and four rows of sweet corn became eight. Cabbage, carrots, beets and tomatoes from our garden fed the restaurant diners. The cake pan was being filled again. We watched Daddy's bank account of cotton and calf money, hoping we could order the wardrobe before he needed our little hoard. But as summer wore on, time and again, Daddy needed $5 or $10. With all these setbacks, it took a long time indeed for the amount to grow.

One Saturday in the fall, Mama gave me a box of money and a filled-out money order request. It was money for the wardrobe and freight charges plus the money order. I sat in the shade of a rambler rose and waited for the mail carrier, hoping Daddy wouldn't come along and ask what I was doing. The carrier lifted his eyebrows when he saw the numerous coins and bills to be counted, but finally the order was off to Montgomery Ward.

After an anxious week or two, a card came from the depot for us to pick up some freight. Mama and I hitched a team of gentle old mules to a wagon and brought home the big crate holding the precious wardrobe. A hired man helped us uncrate it and set it up in the downstairs bedroom.

In these more affluent years, when I store something in the old wardrobe in an upstairs bedroom, I remember my feelings and Daddy's reaction. With a mixture of happiness and apprehension, I showed him his overcoat, good suit and a few starched shirts hanging in one side while Mama's clothes were crowded with my own in the other side. The two top drawers in the middle were given to his socks, ties and underwear, while we used the three bottom ones. I opened the mirrored door to the hatbox and showed him the place we had for his good black hat.

He knew we had outfoxed him. But he just smiled a little sheepishly and admonished me, "Be careful not to slam the doors and break the mirrors. This is a nice piece of furniture, so take good care of it." ❖

Ends Won't Meet

How in the world can I make ends meet?
Can't keep shoes on the children's feet;
Can't buy sugar … the price is sour;
Can't use much electric power;
Can't catch fish … can't afford the lure;
Can't raise a garden without manure.
These modern prices frighten my belt;
I feel like a fox that's losing his pelt.
Someone or something has got to give
If the poor and hungry are gonna live.
Farmer, middleman, merchant, all,
Does anyone hear our hunger call?
Five-cent quarters are all the style;
A handful of them won't buy you a smile.
Pennies are only good for a "laff,"
They're nothin' more than copper chaff.
There's no such thing as a five-and-dime,
Like stores of old, that once-on-a-time
Took in nickels and dimes with a smile,
And rarely ever diminished your pile.
Why are prices still goin' up?
I'd live much better if I were a pup.
I'd have no worries … my ends would meet,
An' I'd be solvent on my feet.

—Stanley Eskew

A Happy Ending

By John Henry Mahan

Back in 1933, I was laid off from the Western Electric Co. for lack of work. I had a good work record and could be rehired when business improved. In the meantime, however, I had a serious problem as to how to make a living.

My landlady agreed to reduce the rent and I tried various ways of supporting my wife and son. I tried baking loaf cakes and selling them by ringing doorbells. I did some substitute teaching, and I tried selling humidifiers that fastened onto radiators. I also headed up a Works Progress Administration (WPA) study of what happened to vocational-school graduates.

Then along came an offer to teach in the New Jersey State Reformatory at Woodbridge. I had the backing of the New Jersey State Education Department and the Civil Service Commission. Major Mark O. Kimberling, who had headed the New Jersey State Police and was now the superintendent of the reformatory, called Trenton on the phone to verify my credentials. And so I was engaged to teach mathematics and correlated science to the inmates.

There were approximately 900 inmates, of whom 200 were scheduled for class instruction. Their ages varied from 21–31, and their crimes from petty larceny to murder. The very thought of being so closely associated with these men was frightening, so I called on Mr. Armstrong, keeper of the Union County Jail and a former guard at the reformatory. He filled me in on what to expect.

I found the work fascinating and the boys cooperative. There were four other teachers in the school. On the wall of my classroom hung large pictures of George Washington and Abraham Lincoln. We opened classes each morning with a salute to the flag. Then one of the boys read a passage from the Bible and we recited the Lord's Prayer. All of this was not required, but Dr. Frank, head of the school, said it was all right.

My students fell into the fifth- to seventh-grade group. We studied from textbooks, from experiments, from craft projects and little dramatizations. We became thoroughly engrossed in following Admiral Byrd and his expedition to Little America. We made models of his planes and village, and to top it all off, Dr. Thomas Poulter, second in command and chief scientist on the expedition, visited the reformatory and showed movies of their exploration.

The schoolwork was divided into morning and afternoon sessions. Of the 200 inmates assigned to the school, 100 attended during the morning and 100 in the afternoon. When they weren't taking classes, they joined the other 700 in the various shops—carpentry, plumbing, painting, shoemaking, textile, canning and foundry, where aluminum signs were made for the state highway department.

Each school session included class work and a recreation period. In bad weather we used the large gym, big enough for two basketball games at once, and a smaller room with Ping-Pong tables. In fair weather, the students went out to the recreation area for baseball, handball and quoits. I played many a game of Ping-Pong with the boys, and Clark Jackson and I had many good quoit games together.

It was interesting how some of the inmates looked at their incarceration. One boy told me he wouldn't stay if the 20-foot wall weren't there. He had me go with him to the athletic director's office to see a picture of his uncle who had been an inmate and on one of the basketball teams. Another boy said he had learned a lot while here. I told him I wished he now knew how to stay out of trouble.

In due time, business began to revive and I was offered an opportunity to return to Western Electric. This meant a big opportunity for me. While I hesitated to leave the reformatory, it meant a chance to get back in my chosen field of endeavor, and I continued there until my retirement at age 65. ❖

My Utopia

By H.M. Stitt

I had found utopia. The fact that the rest of the world was a veritable chaos made my utopia seem a lot less demanding. It was 1934, the middle of the Great Depression, and I was 31 years old. A young man with no dependents back then was in a bad way. Hunting for a job was a total waste of time, as all jobs were allotted to men with families.

Then, in the fall of 1932, I discovered Marco Island off the Gulf Coast of Florida. I was a dyed-in-the-wool fisherman, and there I could make a living with a cane fish pole. There was food beyond belief, including oysters, clams, stone crabs and blue crabs. There were citrus orchards that abounded with fruit for the picking, plus coconuts, palm cabbage, the bud of the palmetto shrub, and the gopher, a highland turtle that burrows much like a woodchuck; cooked with the palm cabbage, it made a delicious stew. And the fishing was beyond my fondest dreams.

There was always a market for some kind of fish. Finding and catching them was, to my way of thinking, the way God intended man to live. The one drawback was that about the middle of May, the mosquitoes, sand gnats and other man-eating insects made that part of the country almost unendurable. I had a partner, the Dutchman (he had another name, but no one ever bothered to use it). We had intended to stay the summer, but on June 1 we called it quits and went home to Michigan.

We faced the prospect of a bleak summer. His parents were farmers, as were mine. We could have sponged a living, but we weren't the sponging type. The immediate future looked dreary indeed.

Fortune, however, smiled upon us when an old schoolmate of mine who had drifted out to Washington and married there told me that if we could get to the Wenatchee Valley, his father-in-law, who was the foreman of a large apple orchard, would give us jobs picking apples. A job where a fellow could earn real money was out of this world. We *had* to find a way to get there.

As a boy of 16, I had done a little hoboing, and we decided upon that method to travel west. We took the car ferry from Muskegon, about 20 miles from our homes, to Milwaukee. From there we rode freights.

The country was full of tramps of every description—thousands, I would say, based on my experience, although the overall picture would no doubt have revealed millions. Many of them had been affluent men in their home towns only a few years earlier.

The first years of the Depression had been sad indeed. Suicides were so numerous that unless they involved celebrities, they weren't even front-page news. Women with children were the first to attract attention as being "needy." Many men decided that the best thing they could do for their families was to just absent themselves. Many of these men became mentally ill. Flophouses and soup lines overflowed.

Railroad crews no longer made any effort to keep hobos from riding. All big cities—and some small towns—had some program for feeding the drifting population of transients. Over and over I listened to men who had not been able to manage their own affairs explain how they would run things if they were sitting in the president's chair.

We were in no great hurry to reach our destination; the apples would not be ripe until mid-August, we had been told. When we entered a city we just followed the crowd. These men knew where they were going. There would be a place where we would be fed and housed. Some restaurant would have a room set apart just to feed the bums (we were not allowed to call ourselves transients). As a whole, the food was tasty and sufficient—horse meat, we were often told, but it was filling, and it stuck to our ribs.

We steered clear of the flophouses. From past experience, I knew that they were probably infested with vermin—bedbugs, cooties, crabs and lice. Somehow we managed not to get lousy. We had a little money, which we carried in the heels of our socks.

I am a firm believer in divine guidance and Providence, and we had an experience that only reinforced my thinking. In a small town in Minnesota, we threw a bunch of grain doors into the cattle car in which we were riding. (A grain door is 2 feet wide and long enough to span a boxcar door.) We gathered a pocketful of nails and, using a rock for a hammer, we built a comfy little sleeping compartment. There was quite a bit of straw in the car; using it and gunnysacks and papers we found, we had ourselves a very neat little sleeping cubicle. We had no baggage or blankets. The nights were very cold and our little nest was almost a necessity.

This must have been more than luck: We rode a dozen or more trains during that 2,000-mile journey, and every train from Breckenridge to Wenatchee, Wash., contained that very same cattle car with our cozy little parlor berth. And of the hundreds of bums who rode those trains, none ever found it and contested our right to it.

We arrived in Glasgow, Mont., on a Saturday evening. A big dam project was in progress there, primarily to furnish work for the unemployed. At that time, Glasgow was just a little cow town, with only a county sheriff and two deputies for law enforcement. When we arrived there, one of the deputies had been killed—and no one wanted the job.

We were told that a company of Marines was coming to take over until law and order could be restored locally. It was obvious they needed help; the riffraff, thugs and muggers were in control. The hobo grapevine warned us not to take a night train west. A gang of thieves was known to ride every train, robbing and killing when necessary. On a grade about 20 miles out, they would leave the train, and a car would be there to take them back to town. We witnessed no violence, but everyone was talking about it. We waited to catch a morning train out on Monday.

At some places we were given money to buy a meal. At Wenatchee we had to go north up the valley to Okanogan, where the B&O Orchards were. Our little parlor car went on west without us. We were two weeks early, and we spent the time eagerly looking the country over. "Fruit tramps," as we were called, were needed to harvest the vast acres of fruit. We got jobs even without telling Mr. Wittley that I was his son-in-law's schoolmate.

We attended a rodeo in Omak, a little town to the north. From our perches on a side hill overlooking the arena, we had as good a view as those with grandstand seats. We lived in the hobo jungle where there were a number of boxcars on a siding, supposedly for the bums to sleep in. We bought a frying pan and used a gallon tin can for a coffeepot. There were many others doing the same thing, doing their cooking, waiting for the fruit to ripen.

Dutch was put to work on what was known as the color pick; I went to work a week later. This was a common practice; one member of a crew was given work that all might eat. We received 4 cents per bushel box. We slept in tents on cots, which were furnished. We were charged $1 per day for board, and the food was excellent. We thoroughly enjoyed those big, well-browned steaks.

One night we were invited to ride down to Okanogan in the truck that hauled supplies. We sat enjoying a pitcher of beer as the truck was being loaded. A man was cutting meat. He had a quarter of beef on the saw table and was sawing steaks. Dutch, who had been a butcher, nudged me with his elbow and said, "Just look at that."

I looked but saw nothing out of the ordinary.

"Look again," said Dutch.

I then saw what he saw. The quarter of "beef" had a horse's gambrel joint. We had often been told we were eating horsemeat, but now that we knew it, we no longer enjoyed those steaks as well.

We were to receive a 1-cent bonus per box if we stayed until the orchard was cleaned. We stayed. We made more than $250 dollars each— a lot of money in 1934. I never picked 200 boxes in one day, but there were many there who could and did. I just picked apples as fast as I could, and when the orchard was cleaned, I was top man with an average of 146 boxes per day.

We rode back to Fargo, N.D., with a gang in a Graham Page touring car. Then we rode freights to Milwaukee, and then home to Muskegon on the car ferry.

We were only bothered in one town, Portage, Wis. The town bulls and the train crew joined forces and attempted to clear the train of bums. We rank amateurs managed to outrun and outclimb them and rode the train through both ways. Why they wanted the bums in that town, I can only guess.

We hunted deer in Michigan without success, then traveled back to Florida and my utopia. Good fortune seemed to follow us. We had only arrived on the island when there came a frost that killed millions of fish. We borrowed a launch and picked up many boatloads of dead and dying fish. The Gant Fish Co. wanted a load of fish to take to Jacksonville. They continued to buy for two days. We expected every load we brought in would be the last, but the gold rush lasted until they had a truckload and we had made $80.

My utopia had come through again for a couple of northern fishermen just trying to eke out a living.

I guess utopia, whether in the apple orchards of Washington or on the warm Gulf coast, was wherever you could make ends meet in the trying times of the Great Depression. ❖

Mother's Definition

My mother always said to me,
"I am as rich as I want to be
If I live in a house that does not leak
And always have enough food to eat.

"If I can have shelter to weather a storm,
And have enough clothing to keep me warm,
And if I can always keep my health,
Enough to be able to wait on myself—

"To wash and iron and cook and sew,
And have strength to walk where I want to go,
Then I will be rich—but not with wealth,
But a person is rich if he has his health.

"Rich people may live in houses so fine,
But can only live in one at a time;
The rich can sleep in only one bed,
And their stomachs can hold only so much bread.

"They cannot buy youth with their silver and gold,
For the years will pass by and they, too, will grow old;
They cannot buy joy when they feel depressed
Nor can they buy health when they're ill.

"There's so many things that money can't buy,
Such as life—when it's time to die,
So if I am healthy and happy, you see,
I am as rich as I want to be."

—Inez Hayes Armstrong

Powder Kegs & Oatmeal Boxes

By Emma C. Johnson

"That's over the goal!" my brother George shouted as the Mother's Quaker Oats box with its pilgrim label rolled over the faint chalk line drawn on the oiled pavement of the federal government highway.

"It is not! It is only partly over!" came the rejoinder.

We had to make up our own rules in those days. After all, an oatmeal box did not exactly constitute a football. And our playing field was considerably narrower than the conventional playing field. But the spirit of the game was there.

Modern youngsters plaintively cry, "I haven't got anything to do!" Having tired of television, they seem at a loss as to what they should do with their time. Back in our day, during the Depression, if any one of us youngsters suggested he did not have anything to do, that situation was soon remedied. There was wood to chop, water to draw from the cistern, lamp chimneys to be relieved of their carbon

soot or kerosene to be gurgled into the ever-thirsty lamps. Everyone could find something to do—and if we couldn't find it ourselves, our parents were always willing to "help" by setting us to a task!

We did find time for play, but our equipment was born of our imagination. The recesses of the mind provided a stimulus for conjuring up whatever equipment we needed to play the game.

Take checkers. We didn't own a fancy red-and-black board that folded for storage. We played on a homemade board cut from the back of an old school tablet, and used a variety of buttons for the checkers. If we were lucky, no one lost any of the white or black buttons. Occasionally our mother would confiscate them to sew onto the blue chambray shirts that always seemed to decorate the shelf of her old treadle Singer sewing machine.

Then there were the games we made up by putting our fingers over the numbers describing catalog selections to try to guess their sequence. Quite often there was a pattern in the numbering system that presented a challenge to figure out.

We couldn't afford commercial jacks to play with, but stones of appropriate size served as adequate substitutes—and using a rock instead of a ball developed real dexterity. It was a challenge to throw the "ball" up in the air, pick up the "jack" and retrieve the ball before it fell to the ground with a thud.

Paper-doll books were unheard of, but the old Montgomery Ward catalogs were a gold mine for boys and girls—and the fashions were perhaps only one season past the latest styles! It really didn't matter as long as all the arms and legs were there. But commercial artists were not particularly cognizant of this fact and frequently overlapped figures; sometimes they apparently thought only the top half of a figure was necessary when, say, a jacket was the product being marketed.

Comic strips were another source for building our paper-doll inventory. Here, complete figures were prized indeed, for cartoonists usually depicted partial figures to carry on the necessary dialogue between the cartoon characters.

The pictures of the Campbell Kids who were shown alongside the Campbell soups advertised in national magazines were a fine addition to our paper-doll storehouse. However, since these came out only once a month, it took a long time to acquire a large number of them.

String was assiduously saved and rolled into a ball. That same ball was measured countless times to determine if it was large enough to be encased in old pieces of leather laced together to make a softball. Our hand-hewn baseball bat was jealously guarded from the elements so that it would not become warped or soaked.

Then there was the old rubber tire swing, precariously suspended from the limb of a maple that threatened to break if too many occupants clambered on at one time. And I remember the rubber automobile tires we rolled up and down the hills and along the straightaway. In my mind's eye, one became a beautiful black mare, galloping across the plains, its silky mane flowing in the breeze.

I was raised on a coal mine way out in the country, and we sometimes confiscated the empty, 16-inch, black metal kegs that had held black powder. When rolled on their sides, they became our teeming herd of cattle.

Merry-go-rounds were available only once a year, when the carnival came to town, but the spinning wheel of a Model T Ford that had overturned out in the foothills made a marvelous substitute. Granted, the circumference was rather limited, so the distance we traveled was minimal, but the basic concept was there. And whirling too rapidly was instrumental in achieving a dizzy sensation.

Our high jump was unique. Two posts provided support for the bamboo rod that could be set at different heights on nails pounded into the side of the posts. Occasionally these supports leaned precariously, throwing the rod out of level, so much so that we contestants loudly disputed whether or not a jump of the claimed height had actually been achieved.

We enjoyed many a delightful picnic out among the sandstone boulders in the foothills, roasting potatoes in embers until they were charred black. I am sure they were more delicious than any of McDonald's wares.

We had a fantastic ski hill, too—a towering mound of black slack from the coal mine. Of course, the thought of having skis was unheard of. But we tied dull, brown gunnysacks around our legs, and they worked splendidly as we slid down the slick piles.

Then there was our marvelous swimming hole—not a municipal pool, but a special hole eroded by time and water under the overhanging branches of a cottonwood alongside the irrigation canal. Evening swims were best, just as the sun was setting. The water felt deliciously warm after heating all day in the sun, and so when the cool evening breeze pricked our skin, we snuggled down into the water and let it caress our bodies.

The real climax came when we uncapped the bottles of homemade root beer that had been "aging" for three weeks in the cool, dark dampness of the coal-mine tunnel. When the tingling liquid tickled our tongues, the time we had spent sucking on the rubber hose to get the liquid to trickle from the 25-quart stone crock into the brown bottles seemed time well spent. As we savored the flavor, even the tedious chore of cleaning the bottles with the black-whiskered wire bottle brush seemed handsomely repaid.

We created countless other pleasures using only our imagination and fortitude. Somewhere along the way, however, today's children seem to have lost that ability to dream up their own fun. If it is not packaged or promoted by television commercials, a thought never seems to provide a spark for meeting the challenge of "I have nothing to do!" ❖

Old Fashioned Goodness by Doug Knutson, courtesy of Apple Creek Publishing

Depression Trap Line

By Joseph S. Hufham

T he Depression of the 1930s was so acute that the Waccamaw Lumber Company at Bolton, N.C., had shut down for the duration. Unemployed men and boys filled the surrounding woods with traps; if a hunter so much as found a raccoon's track, it was news!

But that swamp was roughly 18 miles wide and 35 miles long. It stood to reason that there was a section *somewhere* that wasn't being trapped, and I was going to find that place. Less than a mile south of the mill was a 600-acre cornfield. The company had cut the swamp timber and had grown corn abundantly there for years, using no commercial fertilizer.

The corn crop had attracted raccoons and bears from miles around. But the company had Oscar Croom trapping the bears, and unemployed men were trapping the raccoons. The coons were caught up by now, but bears were still plentiful.

I hit the mainline railroad at the break of day. There was half a mile of swamp forest before I got abreast of the cornfield. I saw deer and bear tracks, but no 'coon tracks. As soon as I drew abreast of the corn patch, I saw a board with white letters printed on it: "Bear Trap Out." That kept me on the railroad. It was bad enough to have soup running thin in the kitchen without having a foot or so cut off by a bear trap, so I kept moving.

On one occasion, I crawled close enough to a bear to smell him beside the tunnel-like path in a bramble patch, but I didn't see him.

Up in the day, I came to a wide section of swamp and found myself facing a cloud with a strong wind breezing in from the south. My weapon was a little brass-lined .22-caliber Hamilton rifle. It was shorter than an average single-shot rifle, with a flat stock and forearm. I'd mail-ordered it from Sears, Roebuck and Co. for $2.50. I was carrying it strapped to my back, but upon seeing the rain coming, I unscrewed the barrel from the stock and stuck both pieces in my shirt with the ends under my belt to keep the little gun dry.

I'd bundled up against the cold, and not knowing but that I'd have to camp out, I'd put on a tight overcoat. I hoped so much clothing would keep my rifle and ammunition dry. I had a few rusty steel traps in a bag in case I found some raccoon sign.

The storm struck like a gale. I leaned forward against it. The drops were large and numerous, so much so that I was presently soaking wet. Above the roar of the storm I heard a loud blast, like a police whistle. It sounded behind me, and my first thought was, *A log train is backing a string of empty cars into the woods, and that was the squeal of a flange on a wheel scrubbing the rail.*

Bears in Tree by Charles Bull © 1930 SEPS: Licensed by Curtis Publishing

I meant to jump aside, but saw no train, so I quickly looked the other way. That shrill whistle had brought me to an abrupt stop, and there, just one joint of rail ahead of me, stood a 400-pound black bear! Had he snorted and made that blast? I don't think so. I think my guardian angel whistled to stop me, because I've never heard tell of a bear whistling like a policeman.

His hind feet were down by the ends of the crossties, his forefeet on the rail. Doubtless he'd been feasting on the company's corn and was fat as a mole. I knew he was a 400-pounder because I'd seen a 350-pounder caught by Oscar Croom, and this was larger. At least he looked larger to me.

He stood, looking at me. I could see the circle of white around his brown eyes. He shook his head at me—offering challenge, I thought. My first thought was of running. But then I remembered hearing an old hunter say that for a short distance, a bear can outrun a dog. Instantly I thought, *No need to run. He'll catch me!* I was tired and my wet clothes had me loaded down.

Already my heartbeats pounded in my head. I could hear it knocking *bing-bing-bing* like a machine gun. I was afraid to start trying to fish out my rifle. Besides, a hunter had told me, "Never bap a bear with that little rifle if you don't want to get torn to pieces. It will just infuriate him and he'll get you."

Another thing I'd heard was, "If ever face to face with a vicious beast, just stare at his eyes." And that was what I was doing!

Maybe that did it. The bear gave me one more mean look and poked off into the swamp, crossing the track to do so.

I waited until he was breaking sticks out a ways, then got out the rifle and loaded it. A few yards farther on I came to what is known as Big Ridge, and from it I could see a bramble bay. I was now out of the swamp, and I walked to where the bay skirted the foot of the ridge.

The rain had stopped. It had washed away tracks, but I found where coons had been eating bramble berries and began stringing out traps.

When I got back to the log, I found that bears had been there and gotten what was left of the squirrels. That helped me make up my mind to try to not spend another night there.

I followed a deer path through the bay and came to a ridge that looked like an old field. There was nothing but broom straw belt high on it, except at the northwest corner.

Many years back, the company had made a skidder set there and a deep hole had been dug to furnish the boiler with water. Around it there had come up a thick clump of pine saplings now 20 feet high.

There had been a long dry spell and varmints had been going there for water. Around the water hole I found the skeletons of five deer, one with pinches of meat still stuck to the bones. I figured that a cougar had caught that one, maybe a couple of days back.

Scared, I went to the other end of the opening and found an enormous cypress log. The swamp joined that end. The log had been sawed in the swamp, then dragged to the hill by the skidder. The butt end was flared like a bugle. It was hollow. The top end was pithy, so the skidder force had left it. The bark had long since rotted away. Rain had washed it clean, and the sun had bleached it. The hull was seasoned, and I thought, *That's a good place for me to spend the night.*

I strung out the rest of my traps. Squirrels were plentiful so I dropped a couple to barbecue for supper. I built the fire close to the mouth of the log because I'd heard that wild beasts are scared of fire. While my squirrels were toasting, I gathered enough driftwood from the swamp to keep a fire going through the night. The only thing on me that was still dry was a metal snuffbox of matches and a Vaseline jar full of salt, so I had fire and salt on my squirrels. And my, those squirrels were good!

The fire dried my clothes and I slept on my overcoat. I crawled into the log backward, keeping my head facing the fire. I've often wondered what would have happened if a bear as large as the one I had seen had come into the mouth of that log. I've since learned that a .22 bullet in a bear's brain will drop him on the spot. Had that bear squeezed in to get me and I had killed him, he would have blocked the passage. The interior of that log was so slick, I never would have been able to push him out.

Owls hooted and bobcats squalled, and once a fox barked, but no bear or cougar came to get me. My fire had died to a bed of coals, sending up about as much gray smoke as an idly burning cigarette.

I was out at the first gray streaks of dawn to shoot a squirrel that was chattering. He was in an oak that had branches over the foot of the ridge. When I dropped him, I saw another, so I got him too. It didn't take me long to roast them. Soon as I ate them, I went to my traps and—great day! I had seven raccoons and a bobcat. I'd baited with salmon. I couldn't tote so much game, so I skinned them, kept the hides and threw the carcasses aside.

When I got back to the log, I found that bears had been there and gotten what was left of the squirrels. That helped me make up my mind to try to not spend another night there. I hit out for home. At Bolton, Hackett Applewhite gave me $8 each for my coonskins and I think I got 60 cents for the bobcat hide.

Anyway, I had almost $57 more than when I'd left the village the previous morning, and soup began running thick in my kitchen. For supper, my wife fixed fried beefsteak, stewed rice, lima beans and biscuits, and to us, the Depression was temporarily over.

We caught up on some badly needed shoes and clothes, and I gave Walter Bordeaux $10 for a used bicycle. I rode it back and forth to tend my traps. I'd found that there were long stretches of the railroad filled in between the ties, so I had but little walking to do.

On one occasion, I crawled close enough to a bear to smell him beside the tunnel-like path in a bramble patch, but I didn't see him. His closeness, though, made me think of something.

Owls hooted and bobcats squalled, and once a fox barked, but no bear or cougar came to get me.

An alligator likes to hear a dog barking; he eats dogs. But all other wild game in my vicinity seems scared if only a puppy barks. They fear a chase, and if they hear large dogs, they'll run like wild deer.

Jim Hopewell had taught me that when I was a small boy. Jim was a good harmonica player, and when he'd play the *Fox Chase*, it sounded like a bunch of hounds, all barking at once. When he would pause, you'd hear a "lost dog" howl like a wolf. Jim would holler, "Hi on!" and the pack would start barking again.

He could stop at a bay and start playing his harp, and if anything wild was in it, like a bear, deer or a member of the cat family, it would often take off in high gear. So I bought myself a mouth harp. That was after I crawled close to the bear and smelled him.

I'd been given a harp as a boy and had learned to play tunes like *Red Wing* and *Casey Jones*, but I had concentrated on playing the *Fox Chase*. That harp became my secret weapon on my trap line. When I'd near a thicket in which I suspected a bear or a cougar cat was hiding, I'd play the *Fox Chase* on my harp.

Once, while up a tree in a bay, trying to find out directions, I played *Fox Chase* and a bear went out of the bay on one side and three deer on the other side. That gave me confidence that the harp was a better guarantee against vicious wild animals than my little .22-caliber rifle.

I trapped the swamp until February. It was take-up time then, so when I went in to sell Applewhite my last batch of furs, he hired me to drive his furniture truck and help his clerk, Clara Russ, wait on customers during rush hours.

All that took away the acuteness of the Depression for me. But I so enjoyed being out in the wilds that I returned three more winters in a row and trapped the great green swamp. ❖

Earning Christmas Money

By John Ray Cofield

Money was scarce during the Depression years, but the desire for it was ever so strong. My two younger brothers and I used various methods for obtaining some money for Christmas spending.

Living in northern Randolph County, Ala., our family lived "hard" during these years. There were the ever-present debts that must be paid, along with the bare necessities that must be bought. The crop money went for these payments, and we were fortunate, indeed, if these were paid in full. Some years it was necessary to carry over unpaid bills. For the most part, however, we paid as we went, we just didn't go in debt. The debts we did have were most likely the fertilizer bills, and for all other things, for the most part, we just did without. There was no extra money for us.

My brothers and I scratched to earn any extra money as best we could. Some years we could pick the scattering cotton, the scraps that were left behind after the last bale of regular cotton was carried to the gin. What a happy day that was! After the last bale was hauled off, we could harvest the stray locks and late-opening bolls that were left in the big fields on our farm.

If it had been a fair, open fall, most of the harvest was over by Thanksgiving time. We could use the three-day Thanksgiving holiday from school (including Saturday) to pick this cotton. Most years it was cold, but we could pick cotton in the cold. If necessary, we could pick the entire boll; then, at night, we'd sit around the fire, empty our sacks, and repack and clean the scrappy cotton. We did this many times.

If it rained, we could not pick our precious locks and the holiday time was lost. We also picked after school and on other Saturdays in December. There was no time to be lost, as we wanted to turn this cotton into ready cash, meager as it was.

Some years I gathered holly, mistletoe and Christmas trees. Then I begged rides to the large town of Anniston 35 miles away where I tried to sell them a few days before Christmas. This was never very successful, but I tried. One year I gathered the holly and left it outside, and the chickens and birds ate all the red berries off it. I couldn't sell it then; people wanted to buy holly loaded with red berries.

It was a great deal of fun "going in business" in the Wagon Yard, where anyone could set up his items for sale. This Wagon Yard was a forerunner of modern farmers' markets. It was an interesting place, where people offered produce and other items for sale.

It was an education of a sort to spend time in the Wagon Yard. Saturdays were the only days I ever "set up shop" there, but I remember the picturesque place fondly. The merchants were all good, honest people, trying to add a bit of cash to the family funds. But the market for any item could become glutted, and it was often necessary to carry unsold items back home and hope for better luck the next trip.

We used what money we were able to accumulate to make the holiday season a happy one. This made the difference in the success or failure of the holiday season—or so we felt. The week we got out of school for the holidays did wonders for us.

How we spent our hard-earned money was of little importance; just having some made all the difference in the world. Most years I used mine to help Santa Claus bring presents for a younger brother and sister and to purchase small gifts for other family members.

There was also the school gift exchange, but very little was needed for these gifts. Many years a nickel or dime gift was adequate, although I think we spent more on the all-important gift for the teacher.

There was just no work available for young boys to earn a bit of money during the "off season." If one could earn some money in one of these ways, he or she was fortunate indeed. We all knew this, too.

Making ends meet around the Christmas season was especially important. ❖

Christmas Angels

By Norman Wall

It was almost Christmas. There was a hint of snow in the air and the ground was frozen hard. Mom and I were alone since Dad had died two years before. I worked a paper route, and what little money I made, I gave to Mom. It was 1931 and there was Great Depression throughout the land.

It didn't look as if we were going to have anything for Christmas dinner that year. But Mom always said, "Son, have faith in God." Mom prayed every night.

The house we lived in was old and drafty and belonged to my uncle, my dad's brother. He allowed us to live there rent-free.

One evening, after working the paper route, I came home to get the coal bucket. It was my job to pick up coal along the railroad track that ran through the middle of town.

I was sad as I prepared to go out to pick up coal. My thin jacket was no match for the cold December evening and we had less than ever to eat.

Suddenly a sharp knock on the door interrupted my thoughts. I opened it and stood face-to-face with two big men. They were not like most men around town; I can't really describe the difference, but they were dressed in new clothes, which was something you didn't see around our town.

One of them said in a deep voice, "We have some boxes of groceries for you folks. Your mother has been praying every night because you folks needed them."

They carried in six boxes of groceries, and on top of one box was a huge turkey. I peeked out the door as they carried in the last two boxes from their new pickup truck. I looked at our old table; it had been empty just a few minutes before, and now it was loaded with boxes of presents and food.

I rushed out onto the porch to thank them, and much to my surprise, the men and their new pickup truck had completely vanished. I stood there, baffled.

I rushed out onto the porch to thank them, and much to my surprise, the men and their new pickup truck had completely vanished. I stood there, baffled. They could not have been out of my sight for long.

Strange things seem to happen around Christmas, and that was one Christmas that I will never forget. We had food that Christmas like we had never seen before. There was a brand-new warm jacket for me that fit perfectly. I wondered how they knew my size. There was even an envelope with money in it.

That was 50 years ago. I now have my own business, and on Christmas Eve, I am busy delivering boxes of groceries, clothing, turkeys, envelopes of money and more in my new pickup truck. But I don't get my information about needy people like those two men did 50 years ago.

I think they were angels. ❖

Joys of the Depression

By Owenita Harrah Sanderlin

*I*n 1932, when prosperity was "just around the corner," I started cashiering my way through college. I had to get a special dispensation under the child labor laws since I was only 15, but at 30 cents an hour, it seemed necessary to get a head start.

The summer before my senior year in high school, after getting my first job, I kept a diary full of ecstatic exclamation points and horrible groans. Here are a few samples of how much I made and how much I spent:

August 24

Ohhh, I am TIRED! I worked 11 hours today, after getting up at 6:30 a.m. I got a horrible backache, but it was THRILLING to do it—I balanced my cash register and tickets for the whole day and earned $3.36!!!! That's worth a temporary ache. Besides, I just had a hot bath and I feel delicious now.

August 28

Didn't have to get up till 7:20 this morning; I only worked seven hours. Just think!! I have earned $17.16 in seven days, working 54 hours. Hooray! The clothes I shall have next winter!

August 31

HOT. Day of the eclipse—89 degrees in Washington. A couple of BOYS lent me their smoked glasses. And the most wonderful thing happened. Uncle Gene took me to the Club Michele after work for dinner and dancing. I wore my long blue chiffon evening gown and red sandals and had a gorgeous time. It was darling of him to take me—it cost him $4. I think that place has the most astounding charges I ever hear of.

September 24

Went shopping with my own $33. Have $13 left. Bought a darling wine dress—I just hope it isn't too tight in the hips. Also bought a wine-colored turban and veil, two pairs brown (kid and cotton) gloves and a set of piquet (sp.?) collar and cuffs. My aunt made me spend $7.50 for a pair of expensive oxfords (which I HATE) when I could have bought some darling sandals for 99 cents. Otherwise everything is GORGEOUS, and I am going to be a KNOCKOUT this year!!!

Although I didn't knock out any boys that year, my senior year in high school, I did manage to earn a half-tuition scholarship ($50 a semester for four years) to eke out my college expenses. I kept on cashiering all four years of college. I lived with my aunt and commuted to campus by bus and boyfriend. (In my wildest dreams I never had a car.)

I fell in love my freshman year while working 40 hours a week and carrying a full load of 17½ hours. I went to all the dances and saw the first halves of all the football games, though I had to leave early to get to work. Dancing in organdy, satin or chiffon in the moonlight or in a sparkly, lighted ballroom, watching your team in the sunshine with a chrysanthemum in your hair … it was so much more romantic than modern dates.

I fell in love my freshman year while working 40 hours a week and carrying a full load of 17½ hours. I went to all the dances and saw the first halves of all the football games.

I also took long walks in the campus woods with my future husband and found time to edit the literary magazine. Another thing we enjoyed that didn't cost a cent was what our elders called "necking"—much more innocent than today's dating scene. According to my diary, that was more fun than anything else, but like the other joys of the Depression, it was strictly limited. Dollar for dollar and kiss for kiss, I do believe they meant a lot more to us!

In any case, there was no question about whether George and I wanted to get married. We did! He was two years ahead of me, and while we were still in the Depression, he went on to graduate school at Johns Hopkins. At his birth a relative had put $100 in the bank for him, and with the interest it had doubled. This bonanza—along with a summer job at the Library of Congress and a full-tuition fellowship—paid his way through three years to a Ph.D.

After marrying him at the end of my junior year, I finished college and we moved to Baltimore so he wouldn't have to commute from Washington his third year. That year we lived on $900. We had a furnished apartment that cost $37.50 a month: living room, bedroom, dining room, kitchen and bath, plus plenty of wild cockroaches and tame mice.

We ate spaghetti (10 cents a package) in canned tomato sauce with hamburger (17 cents a pound); it was delicious, and besides, it was the only thing I knew how to cook. Another graduate student's wife showed me how.

The wealthiest couple we knew gave dinner parties with real (wedding present) silver; they always had beef stew. We laughed a lot, though I seldom knew what at till we got home and my husband explained the jokes.

My husband got his degree in 1938, the year we were struggling out of the Depression. He got a teaching job at the University of Maine for $150 a month—far less than they take out of his salary today, but then we didn't make enough to pay income tax.

Anyhow, off we went to seek our fortune in the fastnesses of New England, poor, but pregnant. We had zero savings (but no debts), no furniture (but two suitcases full of clothes), and each other (all soon-to-be three of us).

We soon made friends with other pregnant couples on campus and kept on laughing.

During the Depression, we were young and gay. We sang songs like *I Can't Give You Anything But Love, Baby*. We bought a Cape Cod cottage on two-thirds of an acre of wild strawberries for $5,000 (our mortgage payment was $45 a month, including taxes). We splurged on a $21 regulation punching bag, a $50 used Steinway piano and three $150 babies. We ate split-pea soup the last three days of the month and gloried in the challenge of making ends meet. I wrote an article about it for *The Saturday Evening Post*, which I genteelly called "White Collar, Slightly Frayed."

But the halcyon days of the Depression finally ended, and we were at war.

Things have never been the same since. ❖

My First Job

By Joan Mavrick

The big event that stands out in my life was the day I was hired for my first full-time job. During the Depression year of 1939, it was difficult to get hired anyplace.

I was trying to get a job at the local shoe factory. I would watch employed people walk by our house every day. To me, they were lucky, working and drawing a paycheck. It was the year after my graduation from high school, and I could not find any work.

I started to do what many other people did: I would walk to the factory every morning and stand in the hallway until the foreman, Jim, walked by. We would ask him if there was any work that day. The answer was always, "No."

This went on for about a month. Then, one cold day about the middle of February, the foreman said that he could use me for a few days because one of the girls in his department was sick. He asked me to walk into his department with him.

I was introduced to a small middle-aged man named Little Jim and a woman named Bonnie. Jim asked them to show me what I was supposed to do. They were trimming the rough crepe rubber from the rubber-soled shoes using large, hand-operated scissors. They handed a pair to me and I proceeded to trim.

It seemed like forever until it was noon. I was anxious to get home to tell my family where I had been all morning. We did not have a telephone, so I couldn't call them. When I arrived home, they told me how worried they had been. My older brother had suggested that perhaps I had gotten a job, but that seemed unbelievable. When I walked in with the good news, they were *so* happy for me. I almost felt as if I was put on a pedestal. And believe me, I was; now I could help with family finances.

I returned to work that afternoon and had very sore hands by the end of that first day. My thumb was swollen almost double from holding the scissors all afternoon. We didn't take a break in those days. Huge blisters formed on my thumb and nothing helped the pain. The only remedy was time. All my co-workers told me they had suffered the same way when they started trimming soles.

I continued working for the next few days. Nothing was said about not coming back.

I did not receive a paycheck for several weeks. I did not even know what my wages were going to be. My associates were as anxious to see my check as I was. Little Jim asked me to show it to him and I was foolish enough to do so. He soon figured that my hourly rate was 28 cents an hour. He told me that I was very fortunate; he thought that 25 cents was the starting rate. Like most people, I learned in a hurry that the $25 paycheck I received every two weeks was soon spent.

On the other hand, my personal wants were simple. I remember when I first spent $5 for a good pair of dress shoes—lovely navy blue pumps—and that spring I also bought a very nice blue plaid coat.

I stayed at the shoe factory until late 1942, when I joined the multitudes who were leaving lesser-paying jobs to go to work in the local war industry. We were hearing stories that leather would be hard to obtain, and maybe we would be laid off anyway. As it turned out, the shoe factory started to produce boots for the government.

By the time I left the shoe factory, my hourly rate had increased to 40 cents—that was the minimum wage by then—but the war industry was paying 50 cents per hour, *plus* monthly and annual bonuses.

But I left many friends behind at the shoe factory. Many of them worked there until they retired. Of course, many of them are gone now, including Little Jim and Jim, the foreman who hired me for "just a few days."

In 1975, that plant was still manufacturing shoes. Many of the procedures had changed, of course, and some jobs had been eliminated over the years by new machinery. Later they built a modern facility, and I went to the new factory's open house and saw a few familiar faces from the old days.

I hope that those who worked there realized how blessed they were to have a job. I know I did. ❖

© *Sunday Afternoon* by Jim Daly

Love Held Us Together

Chapter 6

*I*t was a beautiful summer day, a Sunday afternoon decorated with a verdant canopy of towering oaks against vividly blue skies. Fresh from church and out of my Sunday best, I was lying on my back playing the age-old game of imagining forms in the mountains of the cotton-candy, cumulus clouds.

A creak behind said someone had joined me, so I rolled over, moving my gaze to the porch of our little home. There on the front porch swing was Daddy, already "dressed down," with Mama and my little sister. Mama was playing "this little piggy" on Sister's toes, reducing Sister to a giggling mass on the swing. Daddy, not always given to frivolity, at least smiled at the proceedings.

The love of my parents shined through the reality of that moment, and it crystallized in my mind. The loving tranquility of that memory has stood in all the decades since as a symbol of what helped us survive and thrive. Love always held us together.

No, we didn't have a lot of money. The wolf had been at the door enough times I think we should have adopted him and named him Shep. But the faith we had in Providence and each other—and the love that faith engendered—was enough to keep our family intact and moving forward.

I know the picture changed for each family member from time to time. Perhaps it was Daddy playing catch with me that stood out as the moment of love in my little sister's memory. Maybe my big brother watched as Mama taught Sister to cook, or as Daddy took me hunting with the two of them for the first time. The crystalline moment may have been different, but we all came to the same conclusion: Love held us together.

Love is what drove Daddy to work all day at the lumber mill and then come home to a few more hours of farming. Love is what made Mama give the rest of us the best parts of chicken dinners to eat, convincing us that the back was her favorite piece of chicken. (It wasn't until I was grown and could have any piece I wanted that I discovered her sacrifice.)

The Good Book says that perfect love casts out fear. Well, Mama and Daddy must have had perfect love for us children, because every day of every week of every month of every year they kept fear from getting the best of us, echoing President Franklin Roosevelt's words that the only thing we had to fear was fear itself.

So as true and clear as a church bell pealing in the distance, that Sunday afternoon mind-picture brings peace to my soul. Daddy and Mama and Sister and piggies on an old porch swing. It was love that held us together back in the Good Old Days.

—Ken Tate

Spring 1942 by Grant Wood © 1942 SEPS: Licensed by Curtis Publishing

A Miniature Fortune

By Richard L. Schuller

I was just 8 years old when a thing called the Depression struck our family a vicious blow. It became even worse when my father, a skilled tool-and-die maker was laid off. He and hundreds of other dedicated craftsmen in his Cleveland plant were given pink slips of paper and told to go home.

Mom and Dad had us three little children. When the news was first heard, Mom gathered us all around the old oak dining-room table, and we asked the Lord to help Dad get another job.

We had recently begun buying the new house we lived in and we also had nested away in the bank $3,451.69—a small fortune in those days. Mom kept the tan bank passbook under the sugar canister on the counter. When Mom wasn't looking, I wasn't above climbing on a chair and opening the passbook to look at the mysterious numbers.

I didn't know the wealth the book represented, but I did know that Mom and Dad somehow trusted the little volume it represented. I would reverently place it back under the sugar canister precisely the way it had been for fear that Mom would detect my snooping.

Dad had been given his lay off notice with no warning. There was no severance pay, no paid vacation time to fall back on. Nor was any kind of unemployment check expected.

Had the folks known that the banks were going to fail, they could have taken their money out and stashed it under their mattresses, as some did. They trusted their bank and the federal government. But one morning they stared in disbelief at the newspaper headlines and realized that their nest egg had vanished like so much worthless green paper. Mom stood in line at the bank for more than 13 hours waiting for it to open, but it never did. Never again.

She carefully slid the worthless bank passbook under the canister in hopes that things might get better. Again all of us gathered around the oak table and asked the Lord to help us. As we bowed our heads, I peeked over at Mom and Dad and saw tears rolling down their cheeks. I discovered that day that men know how to cry, too.

It didn't take many weeks before the folks were not able to come up with the $25 monthly mortgage payment on our new house. It was only a month before the man from the mortgage company came by to inform us that the house now belonged to the bank. We had five days to move.

When I heard that we were being evicted, I knew we'd end up around the old table again, and we did. This time we asked the Lord where we could possibly move. When a family from our church offered us a tiny, run-down cottage in their back yard, we moved in thankfully. The rent was $10 a month.

My folks immediately bought some nickel packs of garden seed and planted a huge garden in our back yard. Mom took in washing from a few of the better-off neighbors, and in this way we were able to keep going.

I was of German descent, and my folks talked to the three of us kids half in German and half in English. One day Mom gave me 10 cents and told me to get some *grosse weise bonen*—big white beans. Perhaps I wasn't listening too carefully when I took off for the corner grocery store with my rusty red wagon, for I announced to the butcher, "I want 10 cents' worth of big white bones."

The man looked at the coin in my hand and loaded up my rusty wagon with an ample supply of big white bones, which were wrapped in white butcher paper and tied with a string. Mom was perplexed when she saw that I hadn't gotten the beans, but we had soup for the next four days—and it was good.

My brother Al, who was two years older than I, was forever into some kind of creative mischief. One day when he was playing down by the railroad tracks, he bragged to some of the hobos that his folks were rich and loved to help poor people. He kept telling the men that his parents threw away a beef roast if they couldn't eat it all at a meal, and that his father frequently gave

> *On the ground I saw a green piece of paper that I immediately recognized as a crumpled piece of currency. I ran home as fast as I could.*

dollar bills to unemployed people who came by the house. He bragged that his father would pay $2 to anyone who would cut his lawn.

After Al had spread the gospel about his kind parents to some 15 men, he took off on a dead run for home. He hadn't counted on the fact that these men had believed him, and were very hungry for a partly used beef roast, or better still, a crisp dollar bill.

Try as he could, he was not able to outrun the young, unemployed hobos. When he arrived home, Al bolted up the steps and disappeared in the attic, way back among the spiders and cobwebs, until the storm blew over … or so he thought.

When poor Mom answered the door, she faced a breathless group of men asking for roast beef, dollars or even a job cutting the grass. At first she thought they were crazy. She was about to call the police, but bit by bit, the truth came out, and she told them to wait a minute.

She extracted Al from the attic by his ear and set him in front of the angry men. Fortunately, they now saw the humor of the situation, and they ran Al through a kangaroo court, much to my mother's delight. After the fun was over, she gave them the big vegetable stew she had made for our family supper.

We dined that evening on oatmeal with a little brown sugar on top, while Mom described the escapade to my father. He had been pounding the streets all day looking for any kind of job. Dad was a quiet man, and merely said, "If they had beaten you to within an inch of your life, you would have deserved it, Son."

After over two years with no employment, my father went to work for the Works Progress Administration (the WPA), a government public works program that was, in effect, a welfare effort providing work. The work was hard and the pay minimal, but it was a job, and we saw Dad's spirits perk up again.

His pay was so meager that we still had a difficult time paying the rent and putting food on the table, especially during the frigid Cleveland winters. Coal was expensive, and one February day, Mom paid the last of our money to buy a load of coal. There was no credit then, and the man would only drop the load of coal after he had folded the $5 in his billfold.

Mom wiped away a small tear after she had paid that money. I asked her how much we had left, and she said that there was only 22 cents in change under the sugar bowl.

That night for supper we had potato soup, which consisted of three big potatoes we had grown, flavored with pepper and salt. For dessert we each were allowed one section of a graham cracker. Things were bad.

The next morning, we once again gathered around the oak table for prayer. Our food was gone and we had nowhere to turn but to the Lord. He had brought us through rough times, and we needed His help again. As we prayed, we had no doubt that He would help us.

It was a cold February morning. After we had finished praying, Mom had us bundle up and go out and play in the snow. We loved to do this. But for some reason, I wandered off and walked through our alley, behind a bar.

On the ground I saw a green piece of paper that I immediately recognized as a crumpled piece of currency. I ran home as fast as I could. Bursting into the kitchen, I threw the still snowy bill on the table in front of my parents.

"A $20 bill!" My mother shrieked. "Where did you get it?"

"In the alley."

"Did you see anyone there who might have lost it? We've got to find the owner. He must be very upset!" Mom fretted on and on.

"There were no people in the alley, Mom. Can't we keep the money?"

She looked so perplexed, torn between worry for the person who had lost this small fortune, and thinking about all that it would buy for us.

Finally Dad, a very practical person, said quietly, "Hanna, we just finished asking the Lord to supply us with food this day. He has! Let's go shopping." We all walked to the grocery store, and we bought so many bags of groceries that we could scarcely carry them. And even after our shopping spree, Mom still had $8 left in her brown cloth purse.

After a festive supper that night, we again prayed around the old oak table. But this time it was with full tummies and thankful hearts that we thanked God for restoring hope and at least a little bit of our miniature fortune. ❖

Secret Marriage

By Frances Heaton

I met Paul in 1928 at a carnival in a small school in Nebraska where I was teaching. We had our first date that evening.

By 1937, not only was the country in the throes of a Depression, so were Paul and I. By that time we had been "courtin'" for nine years. I was teaching in a consolidated school a few miles out from McCook, Neb., and was living with my parents. Paul had managed to get a job in that same town and was living in a rooming house across town.

We wanted to get married, but it would take both our salaries to pay the rent and buy food. However, a clause in my teaching contract precluded our getting married. I kept thinking, *Unfair!* Today we would call it "sex discrimination." Finally we decided we had waited long enough; we would "show them."

So, in the summer of 1937, on Aug. 8, Paul and I left with my sympathetic sister and her husband by car for a short vacation trip to Colorado. Since we were with a married couple, people assumed that we were properly chaperoned. We drove south into Kansas, and since it was a Sunday morning, we had no trouble finding a minister to do the honors. Then we went on our merry way out to Colorado for a week's vacation (and secret honeymoon). We spent the first night in a small hotel in Woodland Park. The next day we drove on farther and found a cabin to rent for the week.

When we returned home, I secreted my wedding ring. We were a little apprehensive for a few days as we resumed our premarital lifestyle. But as the days passed and nothing was said, we breathed more easily.

I taught that whole term under my maiden name. By the time I signed my contract the next spring for the following term, we had been secretly married for almost eight months.

School closed at the end of May. Then we called the local newspaper and sent out our announcements. And yes, I was fired—for two weeks. Then the school board had second thoughts. They asked me to return, married or not. The following year I was given the principal's position, and the year after that, the school board asked me to be the superintendent of the very school from which I had been fired.

The marriage clause never again appeared in any of their teachers' contracts. I had made one small step—a very important step—for me, and for other women teachers as well. ❖

Sacks of Coal

By Edward Bergstrom

Folks prefer to remember happy times, but it's good sometimes to recall the "bad old days," too, especially when present life and conditions seem difficult. I always recall the Depression.

I remember the 1930s as a time of grim togetherness. Most families were forced to gather under one roof. The economic Ship of State became as that becalmed sea and craft in the *The Rime of the Ancient Mariner*: "As idle as a painted ship … upon a painted ocean. …"

No smoke was seen pouring from the stacks of industry to pollute the air or feed empty stomachs. Wheels stopped turning and everybody sat down and wondered what to do.

Still, people were friendly and social—in a mutually grim way—with everyone trying to make the best of things. I moved in with Grandma and Grandpa. That was all right with me, as I liked Grandpa. We had problems in common. There we were, flung together by the Depression: an old man, jobless, no hope for the future, and a young teenager, also jobless and frustrated. As an unemployed teen, my problems of adolescence were compounded by an overbearing sense of obligation and futility. I wanted to help and couldn't.

Money was scarce and coal was precious. My grandfather could not always order it by the ton or even a half-ton; it seemed like some sort of holiday when we had a whole ton of coal delivered at once. Generally, my grandfather—a fairly tall but spare man, bent only a little by his years—would go to the coal yard himself and get just a couple of burlap sacks full—300–350 pounds at a time. Pulling and wrestling the heavy, unwieldy sacks on a warehouse truck or dolly he owned, he steered his precious cargo safely through the busy truck traffic of South Chicago Avenue, across 71st Street and down alleys to the basement window of the coal bin. There the cavernous bin devoured the meager load in a single small gulp. It looked a most pitiable pile.

Naturally the coal had to be conserved, fed most judiciously into the furnace and water heater. Consequently there was a lot of complaining in that 13-room frame house on Langley Avenue during the snowy, subzero Chicago winters, particularly from the women—my grandmother, a small, bustling woman with small shoulders and large hips, and my Aunt Esther, who lived upstairs. The women complained for themselves, and also on behalf of the few roomers and boarders, upstairs and down.

The income from room rent and boarding was no real fortune, so my grandparents counted pennies week after week, month after month. Grandma nagged Grandpa to go on relief. Proud, he vehemently refused; nor was he dissuaded by the well-fed, healthy, cheerful appearance of family friends who were getting relief. The affluent were people receiving free groceries.

But even those desperate years had their music—the songs of the alleys. "Hey, yella bannum suhweet cawn here, quawtuh a dozen!" Unemployed, earnest young men and older teens dug out their coaster wagons and pulled them over to the wholesale markets on State Street. There they gambled important investments on small loads of vegetables and fruit, which they hawked up and down the hot, fly-buzzing alleys. It is true that people often bought because they knew some boy and felt they wanted to help—not because they could really afford the quarter.

Other alley songs from those days included the tinny, nasal, weary monotone of the old iron-and-rags man, driving a rickety wagon behind a bony, half-sleeping horse: "Lags-a-lags, lags-a-lags! Any old lags!" Then erupted the startling shout of the iceman!

Simple excitement was welcome. The mere sound of a hammer on a porch board, or the sawing of wood in repair of a fence on a sunny spring morning, perked interest and stirred hope that men still possessed a will to be active.

But things were to get worse before they got better. People worked jigsaw puzzles, but nobody could put the economy together. Smokers rolled their own cigarettes with Target cigarette-making

Pile of Coal by John Slobodnik, House of White Birches nostalgia archives

machines, or learned to roll them with their fingers, using Bull Durham. Men used bar soap for shaving lather and cut each other's hair, or did not get their hair cut at all. Grandpa and I were no different; we went without haircuts and competed for length honors. Once, when I went five months, I could have rivaled today's long-haired fellows.

Chicago's Century of Progress Exposition of 1933–1934 provided some escape and diversion. My family attended and if the irony of progress occurred to us, no one mentioned it. We tacitly overlooked the apparent inconsistency between 100 years of alleged progress and our personal lack of pocket change.

Each of us agreed "the fair" was a good and wonderful thing. It was. For one thing, it gave a job to my cousin George Bengston, five years my senior, who roomed and boarded in Grandpa's house. George worked as a uniformed guard at the Fort Dearborn exhibit.

I went to the fair with my Uncle Gus, his wife, Aunt Terry, and Grandpa. We ate fruit soup in the Swedish Village. The fair ended too soon, and we lost a little of our lightness in the major Depression gloom. Once again, our major diversion became the newspapers.

My favorite reading, at least in September 1935, was about the Cubs, who chalked up 21 straight successes and lofted the pennant. Grandpa knew about the Cubs, too, calling them the "Coobs," but his real interest was political. He always voted—no one took his American citizenship more seriously. On voting days, he rose early, spoke little, dressed up and departed solemnly, respectfully and dutifully for the polling place.

He also liked to walk up to Oakwoods each Decoration Day to hear and see the ceremonies in memory of the war dead. Grandpa's stroll to the cemetery on Decoration Day was also for something to do, in his "off-season" from hauling coal. Hauling coal was his main "retirement" occupation and he clung stubbornly to the activity. When Grandma nagged him to stop, he vehemently refused.

"I drive coal so long as I am able!" he would snap. He did for 10 years, and he permitted no help. He finally allowed me to go to the coal yard with him once, when I was 20 years old. The man who weighed out our coal beamed. It pleased him that we were a team. Respectfully amused, the man smiled. "Old horse and young horse," he observed, "pull pretty good together!"

During the summer, we needed less coal, and so Grandpa's work was less strenuous. His life had been strenuous enough. He had been a glassblower until machines took his trade. Grandpa's way of blowing out his rosy cheeks very large in exhalations when he slept and when he noisily cooled coffee in his saucer was worthy of a glassblower or anyone else.

His trade gone, Grandpa worked for many years handling sacks for a seed company. The sad part of his retirement thereafter was that he was forced to feel unemployed. "Here I go without work," he complained. He was old enough for retirement under normal economic conditions, but he did not feel that way.

Grandma's main province was her kitchen, old-fashioned even that long ago with its old coal-and-gas range. But outmoded equipment did not hamper Grandma's culinary skills. Grandpa had plum and cherry trees in the yard that yielded bountifully, and Grandma would put up the cherries scalding hot in quart glass jars near the end of the summer. Then, in February, to the surprise, delight and mild mystification of the boarders, Grandma would produce the cherries in their sweet, roseate juice, delicious on small, thin, and big, thick pancakes.

In winter, the cherry trees, their branches sheathed in ice, crackled as they moved like skeletons in the frigid breeze. The boarders peeked out at the stiff trees through an ice-free corner of the frozen kitchen window, then returned to the kitchen table, smiling and shaking their heads. They could not comprehend this miracle of preservation that could give them fruit, warm and sweet, from trees now so bleak and cold.

Grandpa and Grandma are gone. Grandpa's physical remains have lain in Oakwoods for almost 65 years, but his dogged spirit still walks. I can hear him yet, a little embarrassed, apologetic, and complaining that the cold makes one's nose run, as he comes into the kitchen out of the ruthless winter. And I can still see him get out his red-and-white handkerchief with cold-stiffened fingers and daub at the offending proboscis.

Though he persevered, Grandpa did not go through those years unmoved by the conditions around him. "I have blues," he complained

> *Money was scarce and coal was precious. My grandfather could not always order it by the ton or even a half-ton; it seemed like some sort of holiday when we had a whole ton of coal delivered at once.*

once. And once, through the partly open door to his bedroom, I saw him, elbows on the knees of his widespread legs as he sat leaning forward, reading his black, leather-bound Swedish Bible. But he endured.

The main occupation of Chicago—and the nation—in those long-ago years was unemployment. People worked at building their patience and struggled to ride out the economic doldrums. We were humbled by circumstances, but we cultivated mutual respect in an effort to provide each other with some sense of dignity as a synonym for hope. And hope was an answer to worry—worry fueled by questions such as, "Where will we get the money for tomorrow's bread?"

We always got it somewhere, somehow, generally when a working roomer and boarder decided, without being asked, to pay his rent a little in advance. Then there was a last-minute dash at about 5:30 p.m. to the grocery store and to Mr. Nelson's meat market at 73rd and Cottage Grove, for a hurry-up supper featuring meatballs and brown beans.

I could remember the Depression by any number of things, but I remember it best by a couple of sacks of coal, and the love of the old man who moved them. ❖

Miracle Mesilla Park

By Vernon R. Harris

The Great Depression in the year 1935 was a terrible blight, which covered most of America. All I knew about, though, was the small corner of New Mexico where we, migrant farm workers, struggled to survive. We were "Okies" and poor ones at that.

As a small child, I often prayed for rain; when it rained, the cotton fields were too wet to work in, and I could enjoy a day of uninterrupted play inside the crude cabin we called home. I was too young and ignorant of the world to realize that work—the cruel, exhausting labor of picking Pima cotton—was all that kept our family and lots of others from starving.

There were no snobs in the cotton fields; black people, Mexican-Americans and whites mingled freely, and all pulled heavy sacks among the cotton rows. All of us—from Oklahoma or Arkansas, Texas or Mississippi—were there at that particular time because New Mexico had a crop that needed picking. The year before we had been in Texas; later some of us would be in Arizona. Life was difficult—especially for our parents—and there seemed to be no sign of improvement on the horizon.

In this situation, in the summer of 1935, life went on. In June, as my seventh birthday approached, I expected little in the way of gifts. I knew how hard my parents worked and how deeply they worried about my welfare and that of my sisters.

It was a great surprise, therefore, when on the morning of my birthday, my father announced that there would be no work for the two of us that day. Instead, he and I would drive his old, broken-down Chevrolet into the nearest town, Mesilla Park. I was consumed by curiosity, not knowing what to expect.

On the morning of my birthday, my father announced that there would be no work for the two of us that day. Instead, he and I would drive his old, broken-down Chevrolet into the nearest town.

Our first stop was the drug store—specifically, the soda fountain, where my father ordered me a heaping dish of store-bought ice cream. He ordered nothing for himself, but simply sat on an adjacent stool while I enjoyed this unheard of luxury. It cost him a dime, which he gravely brought forth from his change purse. I offered to share my great fortune with him, but he shook his head. "No, son," he said. "It's your birthday—I want you to have it all."

Our next destination, across the street, was a hardware store. I was beside myself with excitement as we entered; hardware stores, of course, stock a million wonderful things. People like us, I knew, could afford none of them. Just the same, Dad told me to wait by the front door. Then he walked to the rear of the store.

I could see him whispering with a clerk. Then, smiling broadly, he returned to where I waited, pulling the largest, most beautiful red wagon in the store. This treasure, he said, was mine! None of the several new automobiles I have since bought has ever lifted my heart as did that wagon.

Dad paid the clerk with four rumpled, dirty $1 bills; obviously they had been saved at great hardship for this momentous day. I cried with joy at the knowledge that my father and mother loved me so much. Four dollars, in their grim and burdensome world, was a veritable fortune.

I have received many gifts during my lifetime, some of them expensive. But none has ever meant so much to me as that dish of ice cream and the $4 red wagon. That wagon, as I proudly pulled it from the store, was piled high with an invisible load—the sacrifice of two parents who, in the depths of poverty, still gave their son a birthday present he would never forget. ❖

© *Mud Mates* by Jim Daly

Sibling Revelry

By Roy Meador

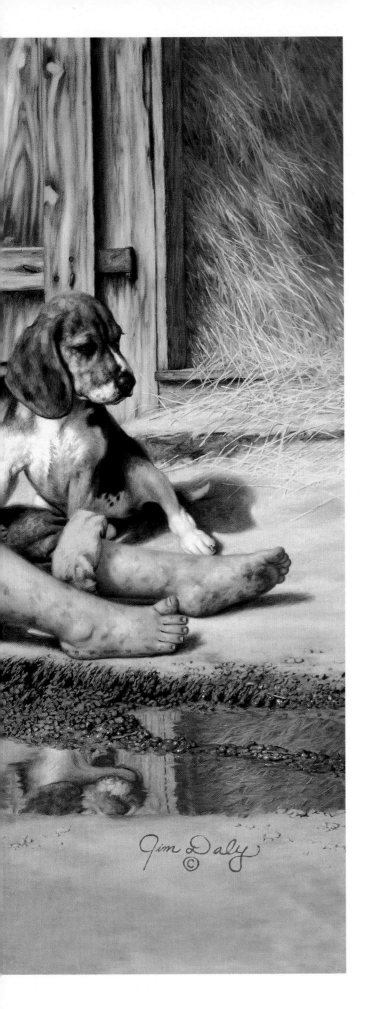

Jim Daly ©

Modern psychologists and sociologists fill books and journals with learned postulating about a worrisome condition they describe ominously as sibling rivalry.

Siblings are people with the same parents. I have two siblings, but I don't typically think of them that way. I proudly call them my sister and my brother. They made the 1930s and 1940s richer and better times for me by being there when I needed them for merriment or support.

When I remember my sister and brother in those years of our shared childhood, the expression that comes to mind is not "sibling rivalry" but "sibling revelry." Happiness and help are what I always received from my amazing and wonderful siblings.

In the Depression and war years of the 1930s–1940s, we learned to appreciate and value what we had. For me that included a loyal sister and a cheerful brother. Even as a boy, that's how I felt about my versatile sister, Wanda (now Mrs. Wanda Miller of Plainview, Texas), and my little brother, Jerry (now Jerry Meador of Tucson, Ariz.).

Wanda joined our family early in the 1930s at Amarillo, Texas, when I was a cranky young gentleman going on 2 who was no doubt put out greatly by the whole complicated business of a new baby coming aboard. I was demoted from exclusive boss of the house because of this noisy new visitor and probably developed a healthy dash of bewildered resentment.

Yet, in the years that followed, I gradually came to appreciate that Wanda's arrival was the best thing that had happened in my life to that point. We soon moved to a country place in Oklahoma, near the small town of Blair. With no neighbors nearby, Wanda became my sole playmate on the prairie.

We invented countless games with elaborate rules. While setting up and playing those games, my sister and I learned the give and take of negotiation and getting along that would help us in the demanding games of life later on.

In tiny towns and rural homes, sisters and brothers served as companions and champions, sources and resources, supporters and accomplices, playmates and helpmates, confidants and chums. Without my sister there in the 1930s, loneliness inevitably would have been number one on my childhood hit parade.

From the start, Wanda and I developed the useful habit of mutual cooperation in work as well as play. When I took on any job with considerable scope, I always knew I had a reliable partner to count on in my sister.

If the job was delivering handbills door-to-door, she started on one side of town and I started on the other. If the assignment involved weeding a garden or chopping cotton, she was handy and ready. Naturally, she received a fair share of the profits.

At least I *hope* it was a fair share. Without complaint, Wanda always let me decide what was a reasonable division of our earnings. She trusted me to do right, which just might have helped make me trustworthy.

When my paper route commenced in the early 1940s for the *Clinton Daily News* at Clinton, Okla., my sister—in all weather—carried part of the route. Even then I knew that my paperboy career benefited greatly from Wanda's dedicated cooperation. That effort and many others would have been enormously more difficult and sometimes impossible without her eager, generous assistance.

> *We invented countless games with elaborate rules. While setting up and playing those games, my sister and I learned the give and take of negotiation*

My brother, Jerry, instantly became the golden apple of every eye when he made a dramatic appearance at Clinton, Okla., on July 31, 1940. Baby Jerry's welcome introduction to the family circle came a few weeks after a cataclysmic hailstorm hit western Oklahoma, smashing windows and roofs.

Many of the hailstones were as big as baseballs, and to our frightened eyes, they loomed even larger. Yet that disaster proved an amazing boon to our family, as my dad, Walter Meador, worked his way to solvency and beyond repairing storm-damaged houses. We came out of that experience better off than we had been before; for us, the storm seemed the omen of an end to a hard decade.

And then, just at that auspicious moment, Jerry arrived—a happy confirmation of improving fortunes.

Wanda and I were already well along the trail to adolescence when Jerry was born, and we instantly adopted him as our all-time number one pet and the world's cutest kid. I was a hearty reader of heavy books at the time and legend has it that Jerry's first spoken words were, "*War and Peace* by Leo Tolstoy."

I'm not certain what Wanda and Jerry would say on the subject, but I know rivalry never entered my mind with either my sister or brother. They were permanent, cherished treasures for me in the 1930s and 1940s when other treasures were elusive and rare.

Thanks to my sister and brother who made "sibling revelry" a pleasure, I was not alone. I had pals and partners on the prairie. I had their help in times of need, and I often shared with them the healthiest human sound of all—laughter.

During my growing-up years, before the century went mad with war, Wanda and Jerry taught me that among the richest words any of us can know are these: "sister" and "brother." ❖

A Penny's Worth

By Lois M. Holmes

Money was scarce in 1930, but my needs as a 4-year-old were small. Back then, a penny represented two pieces of candy. Grandpa fulfilled my need for candy. He worked nights at the flour mill and stopped at our house for breakfast twice a week. My mother was the oldest of his nine living children. He had been a widower for several years and five children still remained at home. His breakfast visits gave him a little time with his oldest daughter and his only grandchild.

Although he went to work dressed in clean white overalls (a requirement at the mill), by the time he arrived at our house they were dusty with a night's coating of flour. He came in the back door and sat on a chair, which Mother had covered with newspaper. As she prepared his breakfast, he turned to me with a big smile and a deep chuckle and said, "How are you, girl? Let's see if I have something in my pocket."

He had the usual penny, and I knew that after breakfast we would walk to the candy store. Mrs. Kirby must have had at least 50 kinds of novelty and penny candies to choose from in her tall, five-shelf glass cases. The candy watermelon slices were a favorite, so I had to choose only one more kind.

Although Grandpa must have been sleepy after working all night, he was patient. He watched and smiled while I looked at every candy. Occasionally he offered a little suggestion when he wanted me to try something new. Choosing that candy was the biggest decision in my life.

One morning when he came to breakfast he changed his routine and didn't put the coin in my hand right away. This penny was different, and he took time to show me the Indian head. Then he said, "If you always keep this penny, you will never be broke."

Then he watched as I put it in my little bank. I didn't grasp the full meaning of the Depression at that time, but Grandpa no doubt felt that I should learn that money had more importance than two pieces of candy. That day he gave me a lesson in saving money.

I've learned that Grandpa was right; I have kept that Indian head penny all these years, and I've never been broke. The penny is now worth much more than a penny at any coin shop, but to me it is a priceless reminder that I need to invest some of my earnings. It also reminds me of Grandpa, two pieces of candy and the love that money can't buy. ❖

Mama & Daddy Would Be Happy

By B.J. Wills

I was born and raised in the Blue Ridge Mountains of Virginia, in Bedford County, not too far from the Natural Bridge, but this fact never impressed me much until I was grown. We could stand in our front yard and see the Peaks of the Otter, which were the highest peaks in the Blue Ridge Mountains in Virginia.

I grew up during the Depression, when times were hard, even on the farm. We always had plenty to eat, but we had to work hard to raise it. I came from a large family; I was the youngest of four brothers, and we had five sisters. Each of us had work to do, and we did it, no questions asked.

Mama cooked large meals every day. We called them breakfast, dinner and supper. Our farm had 150 acres, so Daddy usually hired several hands to work for him during the harvest. Mama cooked for all the hired help plus her own large family—and boy, could we eat.

Daddy mostly raised corn, wheat, hay and tobacco, which was our major moneymaking crop. Of course, we also had a vegetable garden every year, and Mama canned vegetables and fruit every year.

The children kept silent as Daddy sat in his chair by the window in the front room and read his paper.

Daddy was known all around for raising fine tobacco, and Mama was just as well known for her good cooking. With such a large family, it was no wonder she was a good cook, for she got plenty of practice. It was not at all unusual for Mama to bake biscuits and corn bread for one meal, plus prepare two kinds of meat and any kind of vegetable you could name. There was always something for our sweet tooth on the table, too—either preserves or molasses, for Daddy liked to "sop" his biscuits in molasses.

We enjoyed fresh eggs when the hens were laying, homemade butter we churned ourselves, and always lots of milk. In fact, we sometimes had so much milk that we threw it to the hogs. Maybe that's why our hogs were known to be the fattest ones around at hog-killing time. They usually weighed in at 400–500 pounds apiece.

We always had a nice, home-cooked dinner when the preacher came to call, and we also got to go into the parlor and sit. The parlor in those days was what you would call the living room these days. But back in

Relaxing With the Radio by John Slobodnik, House of White Birches nostalgia archives

the Good Old Days, the parlor was reserved for special occasions, like when the preacher came, and was not used much at any other time.

It was furnished with a davenport (which Mama made into a bed for overnight visitors), several chairs and rockers, and our radio, which we children loved to play. There were large pictures on the papered walls of relatives long since gone. We also had a long table we called "the library table" with more pictures on it. I can remember my Uncle Johnny's picture hanging on the wall, and Daddy telling stories about when Uncle Johnny was the sheriff of Howard County, Mo., during the days of Frank and Jesse James. Daddy still had the old star badge Uncle Johnny had worn and his old Colt .44 pistol, and he promised them to me when I grew up.

They were happy times indeed when company came to call. We built a nice fire in the parlor fireplace and spent the evening sitting on the davenport, listening to the radio and eavesdropping on the grown-ups.

We had never heard of television, obviously. We children had our fun by walking to the country store about five miles away on Saturday night, and by listening to the *Grand Ole Opry* on the battery radio. We thought the battery radio was about the greatest thing we'd ever seen, but the batteries were very expensive. We only turned the radio on for a few choice programs like *Lum and Abner* and *Amos 'n' Andy*. If we children were lucky, we'd have a few pennies saved up to buy a stick or two of hard candy to suck on while walking home from the store.

Sunday was a day of rest. We didn't work except for the chores that had to be done every day, such as watering and feeding the livestock and milking the cows. After doing our morning chores, we all dressed in our Sunday clothes and walked to church. My "Sunday clothes" were a clean pair of bib overalls and a clean shirt. In the summer we sometimes even went barefoot on Sundays.

Christmas in the Blue Ridge Mountains during the Depression years was celebrated much more quietly than it is now. We cut a tree and

placed it in the parlor, and the girls trimmed it. On Christmas Eve we children hung our stockings by the fireplace for Santa to fill, and the next morning they would hold an apple, an orange, some hard candy and maybe a few nuts.

We children got some small toy—perhaps a doll for the girls and a pocketknife or cap pistol for the boys—nothing big. Daddy would take the poker and rake the ashes around in the fireplace to look like footprints, then tell us it was where Santa Claus had come down the chimney.

Mostly on Christmas we just enjoyed a lot of good home cooking and people coming by to visit. That was the way we celebrated. Of course, being good Southern Baptists, we thought of Christmas first as a religious holiday celebrating the birth of Jesus Christ. It still means that to me.

Our pantry was a room all to itself. That was where Mama kept all the food she had canned, the fruit and vegetables, the barrels of flour and the cornmeal. We also had canned meat. Our pantry was full all the time. Some of the best meat I've ever eaten was canned and put up in glass jars by Mama. People have often asked me how we kept our food from spoiling back on the farm. All I can say is I'm still alive and kicking, and food just didn't seem to spoil back then like it does today.

Bedford County had a weekly newspaper that arrived in our rural mailbox once a week. Nobody touched the newspaper until after Daddy was through with it, and none of us talked or made any noise while he was reading it. We children kept silent as Daddy sat in his rocker by the window in the front room, which was his and Mama's bedroom, and read his paper.

We always seemed to have smart dogs on the farm. I especially remember one little stray collie dog that came to our house one time. It seemed to like us, and stayed. We called the dog Lady. Daddy soon had Lady so well trained that she would round up the cows with just a sharp command from him. All he'd say was, "Lady, go get them cows in," and away she'd go and bring them home to be milked.

We had one smart heifer that would stand as still as a mouse so the bell around her neck wouldn't tinkle and Lady would have a hard time finding her. She seemed to know exactly when it was time for Lady to come looking for her. But eventually, Lady found her. Then she'd give the heifer's heels a little nip and chase her on home. Guess cows are smart critters, too.

Our house originally had been built by my grandfather and was built of logs. By the time I was born, Daddy had built onto the house quite a bit, so we had more room. Downstairs we had a kitchen, dining room, parlor, entry room, Mama and Daddy's bedroom and a double back porch, which was screened in. Upstairs there were two bedrooms—one for the girls and one for the boys—and a hallway. This doesn't sound like much room for such a large family, but we never seemed crowded.

Wash day was a big day for Mama. I remember it well. Mama put out tubs and pans to catch rainwater, but we boys still had to carry more water from the spring. And the spring was about 250 yards from the house and straight down a steep hill, so you can imagine how we all liked this chore.

Mama separated her clothes into piles— white clothes in one pile, colored in another, then the work clothes, the towels and wash rags, and so on. She washed them on the washboard with lye soap she had made herself, rinsed them in one of the tubs of water, and placed the white clothes to be boiled in a large, black, iron kettle. Then she hung them in the sunshine to dry. Mama always picked a pretty day to do the washing. In winter when the weather was bad, we children were warned to be extra careful with our clothes, to keep them clean, as she didn't know when she might be able to do the washing again.

Shoes were another matter. We were allowed one new pair of shoes a year and they were expected to last all year. But if you were not careful, you might have to wear a shoe with a rundown heel or a toe out until it was time to buy another pair the next year.

We went to school rain or shine unless

They were happy times indeed when we built a nice fire in the parlor, and spent the evening listening to the old radio.

we were sick. We rose early, did our morning work and brought in the day's firewood, ate our breakfast, and went to school. We used a lot of firewood in those days because we had two fireplaces, and Mama cooked on a wood-burning stove.

For breakfast, we had ham or sausage, eggs, gravy, biscuits, preserves and molasses with milk or coffee. Even we children drank coffee with lots of milk and sugar in it. Then Mama would fix our lunch and pack it in a paper bag or lard can or molasses can—usually biscuits with sausage or ham between them, maybe a sweet potato, or whatever she had handy—and off we'd go to catch our bus.

We had to walk two miles to catch the school bus. But I also can remember when we had to walk all the way to school, before the days of the bus came along. Two teachers taught seven grades in our two-room schoolhouse. Grades one through four were in one room and grades five through seven met in the other.

After school we rode the bus back to our getting-off place and then walked the two miles on home, where we changed clothes and got ready to do the night work.

Of course, we had fun, too. We boys enjoyed hunting rabbits and squirrels, and sometimes our sisters joined us to play hide-and-seek and other games in the yard.

My life on the farm in the Good Old Days was not all a bed of roses, but we all felt loved and secure, even though we did not have many material things. We were taught to respect our elders, to believe in the Good Book, and to do as we were told.

I have never been ashamed of my upbringing, and I often long for the quiet moments back on the farm in the Blue Ridge Mountains. Mama and Daddy are long gone now and are sadly missed. But the way they raised me and the things they taught me to believe in will never leave me. They are as much a part of me today as they were in the days I was living with them back in the Blue Ridge Mountains of Virginia. I know Mama and Daddy would be happy to know that. ❖

Little Cowboy Takes a Licking by J.C. Leyendecker © 1938 SEPS: Licensed by Curtis Publishing

Meadowbrook Farm

By Jean L. Woodward Werner

During the Depression years my folks had an 80-acre farm in central New Hampshire. Half of it was woods; the rest was hilly fields framed by stone fences.

These fences were picturesque to look at. In fact, they were only a farmer's way of putting those pesky stones to good use once they were hauled from the fields.

Frost was possible every month of the year. There were times when the corn never ripened and tomato and cucumber plants blackened in a late-summer frost. Dad worked hard, and food was always plentiful, but cash was very hard to come by. At the creamery he got only pennies a gallon for our milk. Besides milk, cream, butter and "Dutch cheese" from our cows, we had eggs, and hams and bacon, which Dad smoked to perfection.

Mama made jelly and canned countless quarts of vegetables for good winter eating. Evenings, she'd play her piano and sing our favorite songs. The piano was her pride and joy and I loved its mellow, bell-like sounds.

Each year Dad cut down some trees, which became firewood to warm us through the long winters. Barney and Chub, our faithful black roan team, "twitched" the logs out of the woods and hauled them home. One day, Dad's ax slipped and cut his left foot badly, right through his heavy boot. My two sisters and I had gone with him that day; we were frightened to see the scarlet blood spurt every time he came down on that foot as he ran home. Once there, he took off his boot, put salt in the cut, and sewed the edges of the skin together with a needle and thread.

At milking time I'd go to the barn with a tin cup. He'd squirt milk into it, right from the cow. That warm, sweet milk tasted much better than cold milk from a pitcher! I secretly yearned to milk a cow myself, but I was afraid Dad would say I was too small. One day when he was busy with something else, I grabbed a clean pail and set the milking stool alongside old Brownie, the gentle matriarch of our small Guernsey herd. I imitated the hand motion I'd seen Dad use so many times,

One day a friend and I decided to have our own little rodeo. With clothesline rope, we each lassoed a calf and climbed on.

and I was ecstatic when a thin stream of milk sluiced into the pail. I didn't hear Dad approaching until it was too late to escape, so I beamed him a big smile, saying, "I like to milk, Dad!"

How relieved I was when he grinned and said, "Well, I'll be!" After that, I milked Brownie many times.

One day a friend and I decided to have our own little rodeo. With clothesline rope, we each lassoed a calf and climbed on. We were merrily racing around the barnyard when suddenly Dad appeared. No grin or gentle words this time! We were marched out of the barnyard, and my friend was sent home. Thus my calf-riding career ended.

In October a few years later, our farm life went up in flames. Dad had hauled some beet pulp into the barn. When he started the truck to back out, it backfired and sparks ignited bits of hay on the cement runway. Both end doors of the barn were open. The tunnel of wind fanned flames into the haymow.

Dad was horror-struck; he couldn't stop it, and any help was miles away. The animals were safely outside, but the barn and house were doomed. The roaring tunnel of flame soon set the south end of the house afire. Dad made a Herculean effort to save Mama's beloved piano. He removed the front door and had the piano halfway out when it jammed and wouldn't budge another inch. Mama cried as it met its fiery fate.

We watched in stunned silence as the house roof crashed into the cellar, and then the tears came. Dad wrapped us all in his arms and said, "It's gone, but *we're* here, and that's what really counts!" How right he was! I knew right then that we'd use whatever resources we could muster and start anew and survive.

Those years on the farm offered priceless lessons in living—about working together, sharing, taking the bad with the good, and meeting life head-on, no matter what. As I look out over the 80-acre farm my husband and I own here in Wisconsin, I know these lessons are just as valid today as they were then, and will be so for all the tomorrows. ❖

Country Kitchen by Doug Knutson, courtesy of Apple Creek Publishing

Thanksgiving Dinner

By J. Virginia McCabe

It was the Depression; we ate a lot of macaroni and buttered bread sprinkled with cinnamon. I was only 10; my brother was 12. In later years I came to understand that he had supported our family of four with money earned from his paper route. The coup in that year of poverty was the meal Junior provided on Thanksgiving.

He was a sturdy boy, wearing his knickers loosely; his shirttail was always slipping over his belt. He allowed his cowlick to stand up straight like a winged bird. Fixing flats on his bike and figuring accounts in his route book were part of his daily routine.

One day he called me aside. "Virginia, we have a big secret. Don't tell Mama," he warned. "You've gotta help me shop. Thanksgiving is coming and we have nothing to eat."

I was a dumb kid who stood in the shadow of my brother's exuberance. If he said we had nothing to eat, I guessed he was right. I hadn't noticed. "I'll keep the secret," I promised. "What are we gonna do?"

"Tomorrow morning," he told me, "we will meet at Bohack's at 10 o'clock—and don't be late." He shook his finger at me.

"I'll be there," I said. My heart was pounding. I was thinking I would have to set my alarm for 8 to get my dusting finished. I went upstairs to my room to look at my calendar. Tomorrow was Saturday—and then five days until the big day.

We met as planned. Junior had a list, which he read carefully to the man behind the counter who was wearing a heavy white apron. Junior ordered cranberry sauce, walnuts, olives, eggs and two loaves of bread. He turned to me and said, "Mama will make stuffing for the turkey."

I smiled. Then Junior told the man fetching his order, "I want a big turkey. I'll pay for it now and pick it up Wednesday before you close."

This arrangement was agreeable. Junior handed me the bag of groceries and told me to put them in his wagon outside. I was beginning to get feverish with excitement. I waited for him outside. When I peeked in to watch, I saw Junior paying the bill. He was counting out large amounts of change.

Arriving at home, we stealthily pulled the wagon into the old wooden garage. Together we hid the brown bag in the back and covered it over with a piece of tarpaper. No one could see it there.

Each day we went to a different shop. At the vegetable market we purchased bright red apples, potatoes, onions, turnips, yams and green beans. The next day we were at the bakery to add a mince and a pumpkin pie to our steadily growing stock.

On the last night we picked up the turkey. It was dark. Junior had a flashlight. We pulled the wagon home together and crept into our hideout.

Now we began arranging all the items in a large carton we had picked up during the course of our travels. With the turkey in the bottom and all those good things piled around it, it looked like a great horn of plenty.

Finally ready, we carefully wheeled the wagon to the back door. The carton was heavy. The apples gleamed in the light of the flashlight.

Junior rang the bell and called out, "Grocery boy!"

Mama cautiously opened the door.

Junior laughed. "Surprise! Surprise! Happy Thanksgiving." He swung the door open wide and lifted the heavy box into the kitchen.

"Wow," he said. "That's heavy." He eased the carton to the floor so that Mama could see all the good things in there.

"Junior! Junior! How can this be?" She couldn't grasp the reality of what was happening.

He began tucking his shirt in and suddenly looked shy. "Virginia and I chipped in for this Thanksgiving dinner." He stood there proudly, giving his younger sister half the credit. He was smiling broadly.

Mama knelt next to the box and wept. As she came to her feet, I felt her wet tears on my forehead as her arm encircled my shoulders. She reached for Junior and the three of us embraced. By now, I was in tears too.

My throat still tightens when I recall that scene. My brother looked 9 feet tall to me. And I became a woman that night, 10 going on 18. In those precious moments, I learned about love, caring and the true meaning of Thanksgiving. ❖

Moving to the Country

By James Baynham

When the Great Depression deepened in the 1930s, hardly a family failed to feel its economic impact. Ours was no exception.

My dad had started his insurance agency three years earlier, and with his natural enthusiasm and energy it had done well. It was a blow to his dreams when clients began losing their jobs. With no money to pay premiums, their policies lapsed, and Dad's business failed.

My folks cut expenses everywhere they could. Clothing was patched, and then the patches were patched before the clothes finally were passed on to a younger cousin. The clothes I received from older cousins also had patches that were patched.

Dad cut out his brown-bottled, yeasty-smelling home brew, and Mom's midafternoon 5-cent Coca-Cola was no longer affordable. Many chores had been done by hired help; now the mowing and ironing were done by my parents and me.

In another cost-cutting effort, we moved to Judge and Mrs. Hughes' massive, white, two-story house a mile away. Since the Hughes' upstairs rooms were furnished, my parents sold our furniture.

My grandparents lived at the edge of a small village that was still "early American" in the 1930s. We had visited them before, and my happy memories of their small farm shortened the trip.

It was a small comfort to Mom to be able to keep the radio that Dad had given her only the Christmas before. It was a Majestic, a beauty on long legs, with double cabinet doors guarding its control knobs and lighted dial.

The other furniture was taken away by various buyers. Beds, chests, tables, the kitchen stove—everything was sold for cash. It was plain to see, even for an 8-year-old: The pain of failure was a heavy burden for both my parents.

When it became apparent there would be no relief for Dad in his search for a job, he accepted the inevitability of a move from the city to my grandparents' place in the country.

With heavy hearts my parents prepared to resettle their family. A sadness settled in our home whenever moving plans were discussed. Conversations suddenly ended when my 5-year-old brother, Tommy, and I came into the room. But we heard enough to know that we would not be able to continue living as we had. Even with that knowledge, I didn't feel threatened or sad about moving, though I knew I would miss Mrs. Hughes' books.

My secret treasures were inside Mrs. Hughes' books. A dark cherry-wood bookcase, waxed to a high sheen, stood in her living room. Behind panes of glass, three shelves held leather-bound editions of children's classics.

The black print on gleaming white pages edged with gold held stories of giants, forests, children, wolf dogs and faraway lands. Their black-and-white pictures fueled my imagination.

Whole sections featured epic poems of sailors, Indians, heroes and heroines.

The bookcase and its secrets lured me daily. I forgot the pain my parents were feeling when the smell of leather, paper and furniture polish filled the air as I opened the glass doors. I missed those books when I left them behind. Sometimes I feel I can still smell them. I will *always* miss them.

Trimming the Pie by J.C. Leyendecker © 1935 SEPS: Licensed by Curtis Publishing

Our move to the country demanded sacrifice from all of us. Nothing could be left behind, but since everything could not be carried in a Model A Ford, much had to be discarded. Hard times prohibited hiring a moving van or even renting a truck.

Our remaining belongings either went into the car, on top of it, or were strapped onto the back. Everything else had to be carried on our laps or it wouldn't make the trip.

Mom's radio was tied on top. Clothes, shoes, family pictures, a few toys, dishes, fishing gear, books, a tool box, Dad, Mom, Tommy and I were tightly packed into the old car. Mom packed a traveling lunch but Tommy and I ate all our butter-and-sugar sandwiches before we were out of town.

My grandparents lived at the edge of a small village that was still "early American" in the 1930s. We had visited them before, and my happy memories of their small farm shortened the trip, allowing me to forget the hot summer wind blowing through the car windows.

I was excited when we approached the river crossing. Dad drove through the bottomland to the ferry landing. The small ferry was only big enough for two cars. The other "car" turned out to be a wagon pulled by a team of mules.

A steel cable had been strung from the landing to the far bank, allowing the operator and the male passengers to pull the craft through the strong current to the opposite side. When we drove off the rocking ferry onto the gravel landing, our destination was near.

My grandparents' house was connected to electrical power by a quarter-mile of sagging wires hanging on slightly crooked poles. But Grandma wouldn't allow the expensive electricity to be used for lights, fans or radios except on very rare occasions.

Mom said that since this would be our first night there, Grandma would probably allow the electric lights. But not tomorrow night. When she said she hoped her mother would allow her to use her radio, Dad said he would find enough money to pay for the electricity it used.

As we neared the farm, I was enjoying memories of Grandma and Grandpa. I knew they loved me. But it was a sad homecoming for my parents as they pulled up the long, deeply rutted gravel road. Dad's usual enthusiasm had him wearing a cheerful face, but it only partially concealed the wounds he had suffered at the hands of the Depression.

For my grandparents, the sight of our old Ford arriving only slightly altered their daily pace. The screen door slammed behind Grandma as she came out of the kitchen and walked slowly toward the car. Her body rocked from side to side on heavy, arthritic legs. Strength and loving-kindness arrived at the car with her, relieving my parents' apprehension of loading their burden upon her.

Grandpa, plowing furrows in the distant garden, only waved and shouted "Hello!" since the mule pulling the plow through the rich loam was determined to continue its advance to the far fence. But my aunt ran from the house with arms wide to express her joy at having her sister "come home" to share happiness and sorrow. I was hugged, held, bragged about and forgotten.

Tommy was still a little kid, so he remained in the happy circle, but I could see chickens and pigs and a cow on the other side of a fence. I headed toward them to investigate, leaving the noise of welcome and the adult world behind me.

The lingering scent of Mrs. Hughes' books was replaced by the aroma of new-plowed earth, freshly mowed grass and dry, dusty grain scratched by the quick claws of rust-red chickens.

A dank, musty smell of mud rode the breeze from the direction of the hog pens. Anticipation and curiosity filled me; it would continue to hold me during the years we lived on the farm.

We seemed to have left the Depression in the city to work out its problems without us. I felt good and turned to see if I could share the pleasure with my folks. Across the wide lawn, they were laughing and talking. I could see they felt good, too. I knew then that the love of our extended family would see us through the tough times yet to come. ❖

Across the wide lawn, my parents were laughing and talking. I could see they felt good, too. I knew then that the love of our extended family would see us through the tough times yet to come.